# Teaching
# ADVANCED
# LEARNERS
## in the General
## Education Classroom

# Teaching
# ADVANCED LEARNERS
## in the General Education Classroom

## DOING MORE WITH LESS!

Joan Franklin Smutny • S.E. von Fremd

CORWIN
A SAGE Company

**CORWIN**
A SAGE Company

FOR INFORMATION:

Corwin
A SAGE Company
2455 Teller Road
Thousand Oaks, California 91320
(800) 233-9936
Fax: (800) 417-2466
www.corwin.com

SAGE Ltd.
1 Oliver's Yard
55 City Road
London EC1Y 1SP
United Kingdom

SAGE India Pvt. Ltd.
B 1/I 1 Mohan Cooperative
Industrial Area
Mathura Road, New Delhi 110 044
India

SAGE Asia-Pacific Pte. Ltd.
33 Pekin Street #02-01
Far East Square
Singapore 048763

Acquisitions Editor:   Jessica Allan
Associate Editor:   Allison Scott
Editorial Assistant:   Lisa Whitney
Production Editor:   Veronica Stapleton
Copy Editor:   Codi Bowman
Typesetter:   C&M Digitals (P) Ltd.
Proofreader:   Dennis W. Webb
Indexer:   Molly Hall
Cover Designer:   Scott Van Atta
Permissions Editor:   Karen Ehrmann

Copyright © 2011 by Corwin

Printed in the United States of America

*Library of Congress Cataloging-in-Publication Data*

Smutny, Joan F.

Teaching advanced learners in the general education classroom: doing more with less!/Joan Franklin Smutny, S.E. von Fremd.

p. cm.
Includes bibliographical references and index.

ISBN 978-1-4129-7545-2 (pbk.)

1. Mainstreaming in education—United States. 2. Inclusive education—United States. 3. Gifted children—Education—United States. I. Von Fremd, S. E. II. Title.

LC1201.S58 2011

371.95'2—dc22                    2011012436

This book is printed on acid-free paper.

11 12 13 14 15 10 9 8 7 6 5 4 3 2 1

# Contents

# Acknowledgments

This book is not the work of two authors. It evolved from the life experiences of the many classroom teachers who so generously shared their stories of struggle and success on behalf of advanced learners. Their lives speak volumes to us about the amazing resourcefulness of teachers, who, despite the mounting pressures and responsibilities they face in their classrooms every day, still manage to care for the students who need something different. Their stories inspired the creation of this book.

We also wish to acknowledge the generous support and meticulous attention to detail shown by editor Jessica Allen, as well as by Lisa Whitney, Veronica Stapleton, Allison Scott, and others at Corwin and Sage Publications. They brought the highest standards of publishing to the production of our book and carefully guided us through each phase of the process. For their many kindnesses, we cannot thank them enough.

Ted Altenberg
Gate Resource Teacher
Pajaro Valley Unified School District
Santa Cruz, CA

David Callaway
Eighth-Grade Language Arts Teacher
Rocky Heights Middle School
Highlands Ranch, CO

Marcia Carlson
Sixth-Grade Teacher
Crestview Elementary School
Clive, IA

Scott Currier
Math Teacher
Belmont High School
Belmont, NH

Shelly Docherty
Fifth-Grade Teacher
Glendale Elementary
Vero Beach, FL

Melanie Donofe
National Board Certified Gifted Education Teacher
Liberty Elementary School
Weirton, WV

# About the Authors

 **Joan Franklin Smutny** is founder and director of the Center for Gifted in Glenview, Illinois. She directs programs for thousands of gifted children in the Chicago area annually. She also teaches creative writing in many of these programs as well as courses on gifted education for graduate students at National-Louis University. She is editor of the *Illinois Association for Gifted Children Journal*, and a regular contributor to *Understanding Our Gifted, Gifted Education Communicator, Gifted Education Press Quarterly*, and *Parenting for High Potential*. She has authored, coauthored, and edited many articles and books on gifted education for teachers and parents, most recently *Differentiating for the Young Child*, second edition (2010), *Manifesto for Gifted Girls* (2010), *Igniting Creativity in Gifted Learners, K–6* (2009), *Acceleration for Gifted Learners, K–5* (2007), *Reclaiming the Lives of Gifted Girls and Women* (2007), and *Underserved Gifted Populations* (2003). In 1996, she won the NAGC Distinguished Service Award for outstanding contribution to the field of gifted education.

 **S. E. von Fremd** is an independent scholar, writer, and editor with a background in education, cultural studies, and dance. She performed with the Never Stop Moving Dance Company in Chicago under the direction of Reynaldo Martinez and taught creative dance and theater to children in the city and surrounding areas. Her interest in creativity and culture eventually led her to receive a doctorate in performance studies at Northwestern University. This included a year's research in Uganda, where she focused on the role of the arts in reviving cultural identity and educating children and young people throughout the country. She collaborated with Joan Smutny on the first and second editions of *Differentiating for the Young Child* (2004; 2010) as well as on *Igniting Creativity for Gifted Learners, K–6* (2009).

# Introduction

This book is for teachers who would like to do more for advanced students but feel unequipped to do so. This may be because of time constraints, a perceived lack of information on gifted education, or the loss of funding that once provided helpful resources for teachers. Whatever situation you face, this book offers quick and immediate help in supporting your efforts to assist students who need more than the regular curriculum can provide. The idea for the book emerged because we kept seeing the struggles of teachers who wanted to assist these students but felt overtaxed by their other responsibilities. Frequently, in workshops or seminars or in private emails, we would hear such comments as the following:

> "What can I do right now in the class I've planned for tomorrow?"

> "What do I do about this kid who finishes everything in half the time as everyone else?"

> "How can I be expected to adjust every single thing we're doing?"

> "Do you have anything we can use in this school that doesn't require reading a long textbook with complicated instructions that only someone with no other responsibilities could possibly do?"

> "We're desperate in this school. We lost our funding for gifted kids, and because parents are upset, the principal is now pushing us all to differentiate more. Is there a way to simplify this?"

> "I'm not an expert in gifted, and I don't have time to become one so I can help the three kids in my class who need it."

While we are not suggesting that an entire field can be conveniently boiled down to a few tips, we feel there is a great need today for some simply stated principles that any teacher can use without having to take a course in gifted education, redesign a curriculum, or attend multiple workshops to understand. This volume has a far less ambitious goal: to offer a guide of proven strategies that teachers can tailor to the needs of their advanced students in a way that is both manageable and appropriate to their circumstances. In many cases, particularly those that involve creative processes, these strategies have the added benefit of extending the education of *all* students, not just those who learn quickly.

The book assumes that readers have little time, few funds in their schools for gifted education, and might have little training as well. It further assumes that readers care not only about children struggling to keep up but also about those on the other end of the spectrum—the ones who seem eager to do more but rarely have the chance to develop their gifts. The benefits of this volume are the following:

- Its brevity! Each chapter is short and to the point to accommodate the schedule of busy teachers.
- It challenges the deficiency mentality of "not enough money, time, or expertise." So what? Some things you do well, and you can assist advanced learners in your class.
- It starts with you, the teacher—your unique abilities, your circumstances, your students—rather than forcing you to reach goals that, for the present at least, are not realistic or practical.
- It helps you create a reasonable and workable plan that will benefit not only your fast learners but everyone else as well.
- It helps you focus on what *you* would like to do in your classroom. In an ideal world, what would you like to do? The book helps you take a small piece of that ideal and do what you can.
- It provides simple ways that you can engage students, vary levels of challenge for different ability levels, and find appropriate resources.
- It demonstrates how effective and inspiring creative strategies can be—how well they integrate into existing lessons, relate to curriculum standards, and benefit children at all levels.
- It also shows how to tackle more ambitious projects for advanced learners in *manageable ways*. Doing independent studies, reader's theater productions, or any other long-term endeavors need not demand an inordinate amount of planning and organizing.
- It offers examples of strategies from classroom teachers that stimulate advanced learners to think more critically and apply their abilities in new ways. Subjects include language arts, social studies, math, science, and the arts.

Credit for this book is due to the teachers who shared their lives with us—not only those who explained what they do for advanced students but also those who reported some frustrations they faced. "So much of what I read or learn in a workshop could only work in an ideal setting," one told us. This sentiment surfaced repeatedly, and brought us to this question: Is it possible to provide ways to support the advanced students without studying long treatises on the subject, without workshops (which schools cannot always provide), without major reorganizing of one's classroom? The answer is yes. However, this brings us to another question: What does it mean to support advanced students?

The eight chapters in this book attempt to answer this question. The first three look at the immediate circumstances of classroom teachers—both the challenges they face and the resources and possibilities at their fingertips. Chapter 1, "Understanding Advanced Learners" provides practical insight into the needs of advanced learners and how we, as teachers, can respond to them, despite limited human and material resources, planning time, and other challenges. Chapter 2, "Making the Most of Your Resources" focuses on *what we already have* (rather than what we lack) and on how we can use existing resources to expand learning opportunities for those who most need them. Coming from the classroom, these strategies can immediately meet, at least, some needs of advanced students, can often enrich the classroom for all students, and can do this without causing undue stress on our time and resources. Chapter 3, "Creating Appropriate Goals for Advanced Students," explores how we can determine reasonable and workable goals for helping advanced students. Examining the different educational needs these learners have, the chapter guides us in deciding what we can *reasonably do* for them in our present circumstances.

Chapter 4, "Meeting the Needs of Advanced Students: Strategies to Begin," and Chapter 5, "Meeting the Needs of Advanced Students: Strategies to Extend Learning," clearly delineate the progression from simpler to more complex adjustments for advanced learners. The goal is to show how, through the simplest adjustment in a source or thinking process, we can immediately create more challenge for gifted students. From these simpler changes, we develop the confidence and flexibility to attempt larger projects that can potentially benefit *all* our students. Being able to shift between simpler to more complex strategies is an important skill today. Teachers quickly need to be able to determine how they can tailor an assignment for more advanced learners in one lesson and then, in another, develop a more ambitious plan (e.g., an independent study or an integrated arts process). These strategies become more evident in Chapter 6, "Teaching Advanced Students in Language Arts and Social Studies," and Chapter 7, "Teaching Advanced Students in Science and Mathematics."

The book concludes with Chapter 8, "Keeping Yourself Inspired." We wanted to include this chapter because, in the stories shared by teachers, we found so many were challenged to find time to replenish themselves. Many said that the students fed *them*, gave them energy and inspiration. Nevertheless, the daily demand to prepare students for standardized tests and ensure that they all achieve a prescribed level of competence in all subjects wore on their spirits. This chapter suggests some helpful ways for teachers to step back from the fray and consider the things in their lives that revive and inspire them. Returning periodically to these sources keeps their imaginative powers alive and nurtures their growth in the classroom.

We hope this book will be a helpful guide for teachers, not a stern taskmaster requiring that they give up their peace of mind to find a path they can follow. All educators who care for the untapped talent in our schools and feel the tragedy of its loss in the hurried pace of defensive schooling want to do something. Yet they also have to "be real," as one teacher put it, about their circumstances and responsibilities not only to the other students but also to administrators and parents. This book acknowledges the realities that many teachers face but also asks, Where are the opportunities? Where are the cracks in the window, the little open doors, and the sparks of interest that can ignite the imaginations of young minds? It offers what we hope will be helpful responses to two pertinent questions: What can we reasonably do? And are we doing it?

Theodore Roosevelt put it aptly when he said,

*"Do what you can,*

*with what you have,*

*where you are."*

# Understanding
# Advanced Learners

In any kind of teaching, we always begin with what the students bring to the classroom—their level of skill and knowledge, their abilities and talents, their deficits, their learning styles, and their interests. No matter how many curriculum guides fill their files or how many times they have to bend to a new policy or procedure from their district, conscientious teachers are guided most by the needs they see right in front of them. They walk into their rooms and immediately know that Maya will probably know half the answers without instruction; that Billy will be at work on his latest cartoon (when he really should be practicing his math skills); that Nehir, a new arrival from Turkey, will turn in twice as much work as necessary because her parents want her to make a good impression; and that Jason's homework will look like he it did during recess (which he often does).

Advanced learners need many things. They need *acceleration* so that they can progress through the curriculum at their learning pace, which is significantly faster than those at their grade level. They need at least some *creative experiences* so that they can experiment, invent, and apply what they've learned. They need materials with which to work their ideas and explore new lines of inquiry. Many also need *sensitive handling*, as they may feel socially isolated because of their passion for learning.

These are a great many demands, particularly for teachers already pressed for time and resources. It might be that their district has no commitment to advanced learners and little funding to support teachers who want to help them. It might be that the focus on achieving proficiency—a legacy of the No Child Left Behind (NCLB) Act—has made kids who exceed proficiency a lower priority. Or it might be that the economic downturn has proven hazardous to districts that once funded gifted education. Teachers who care about this population live in difficult times. They cannot allow these children to slip through the cracks untended by a system that claims to educate *all*. So they try to create manageable ways to make adjustments where they can—often juggling multiple learning needs in one classroom.

This is not new. Since the days of the one-room schoolhouse, teachers have had to become flexible in responding to different levels of ability, knowledge, and skill. The difference is that today's teachers come under considerably more regulation and scrutiny. The moment they enter the classroom, they have to face a predetermined curriculum, mandated benchmarks for student achievement, and a system of testing that often precludes much more than test preparation in the weeks preceding it. This is not to diminish the importance of curriculum development and accountability. But it must be admitted that tests often fall short of measuring what they set out to measure. A poor-performing school can undergo a transformation in revitalizing its teachers, mobilizing its parent base, and increasing student achievement and still find itself falling short in test scores. It must also be admitted that teachers, pressed from every side to cover the required content so that students achieve minimum competence, can often do little more. What Toni Morrison (1996) has called "our busied-up, education as horse-race, trophy-driven culture" (p. 13) sets the tone and pace of our schools. Survival becomes the goal rather than the vibrant, lively art of teaching and learning.

## FACTORS THAT HINDER THE RECOGNITION OF ADVANCED LEARNERS

"What is the largest challenge you face in trying to meet the needs of advanced students?" We've been asking this question to Chicago-area teachers during the past year. Here are some of their responses.

> "Human resources are definitely a problem in our district. We are trying to get a good program for gifted students set up, but the district is unwilling to hire new staff to help fill the positions needed to meet the board/community's expectations."

> "Our district does not recognize nor offer programs for gifted students until they reach fourth grade. Admission is mainly based on test scores rather than input from other sources. Albert Einstein wouldn't have made it in the program!"

"Sadly, I think limited human/financial resources are beginning to take their toll in our district. Schools who have fewer children identified are seeing their services greatly reduced. The identification process has been streamlined, which may cause some children to be missed. I am fortunate to be at a building that has more children identified and a very supportive administrator, but districtwide, I'd say it's resources."

"Lack of planning time to assist advanced learners while I am also meeting the needs of lower and average students. I don't have any help in my classroom so it's hard to balance all the different levels of students."

"The focus in many schools is on struggling learners rather than challenging the advanced learners. NCLB has created an unequal focus on improving test scores rather than providing enrichment opportunities. This causes many high-performing students to be overlooked."

"Top three challenges include the following: (1) insufficient parent involvement, (2) the need for community support programs for the gifted (both for the adults and children), and (3) a lack of networking among schools on the west side (inner-city Chicago) about what kinds of gifted programs their schools offer."

Teachers cite various challenges to knowing and responding to the needs of advanced students, but the following are among the most common:

*Time spent on testing.* The high-stakes testing in many districts means that teachers often feel they can't breathe much until after they've administered the tests. Since advanced learners generally achieve higher scores, they seem better off than those who do not.

*Curriculum restrictions.* Teachers work in prescribed content with benchmarks already established for moving students through the curriculum. Most teachers are quite expert at adjusting things as they go along. But every teacher feels the pressure to bring students to the same level of mastery in all required content areas so that they enter the next grade with the skills and

---

**Common Complaints About Standardized Testing (Schrag, 2000)**

- The pressure for high test scores kills innovative teaching and curricula by galvanizing schools to focus on test preparation in the months preceding exam time.
- Standards on which the tests are based are too vague.
- Tests are unfair to poor and minority students as well as those who don't test well.
- Tests overstress young children and are often too long.
- Low test scores result in punishing consequences, whether or not a school is improving the quality of education.
- Children can't discover things for themselves when the focus shifts from active learning to the test-taking skills.
- Standardized tests don't measure what students really know and what they can do.

knowledge they need. This pressure is often a restraint on alternatives: creative processes, independent or small-group projects, and cluster groups.

*Funding.* It is no surprise that, in the present economy, funds for gifted education have declined and, in some communities, entirely evaporated. This means that the services, whether in the form of a gifted teacher, coordinator, or a pullout program, may no longer be relied on to assist gifted learners. Teachers who are accustomed to a specialist handling advanced students don't see themselves as equipped to pick up the slack.

*Knowledge.* Another hurdle teachers face is the concern that they lack expertise in gifted education or that advanced students need more than they can provide. Exposure to gifted education is helpful, but not necessary. Providing opportunities for them to experience real challenge and advance at the level of their ability is a matter of designing choices that allow for more accelerated learning, creative thinking, and interest-based projects. Many teachers do this to some extent already—by finding areas in their curriculum where they can increase the level of difficulty for more advanced learners. Others arrange for students with particular gifts to study a subject in a higher grade, or they locate parent-mentors willing to work with students on independent study projects related to the curriculum.

*Resources.* Frequently, the material and human resources are lacking or seem to be so. High-ability learners need different kinds and levels of source materials that allow them to expand their imagination and hunger for knowledge. When assisting them, teachers have to consider the range of material resources in their rooms and how well they provide for advanced students. Human resources are equally important. Teachers, parents, community members, artists, scientists, writers, and others can offer enrichment, project ideas, guidance, and practical assistance in the classroom, all of which benefit advanced students.

*Attitude.* Teachers who want to help advanced students often face resistance from peers or administrators because of a bias against gifted education in general. This comes in different forms. "Gifted kids don't need as much as other kids" is one. Another is, "Why should we spend time and money on such a small percentage of our student body?" The first argument—that advanced students don't need as much as others—assumes that care for students who are not learning should only occur on the lower end of the spectrum. Advanced students spend a lot of time repeating what they've already learned or waiting for others to catch up, a situation that can cause real harm over time (Colangelo, Assouline, & Gross, 2004). The second argument—that we should not spend much time or money on a small percentage of students—would never be said about low-achieving students. All students deserve to learn, whoever they are and whatever challenges or abilities they possess.

> ### Do you think that gifted learners should be a priority?
>
> Consider these facts (Turner, 2009):
>
> - Federal funding focuses primarily on helping kids, especially struggling kids, reach basic proficiency. Since gifted students typically exceed proficiency, the schools have little incentive to challenge them, especially as they could face serious consequences for not meeting NCLB goals.
> - Compliance with the NCLB law has increased the trend to starve the already meager budgets for gifted education. Only 23 states have funding for gifted children in this country. More than half of them (13) eliminated the funding in the 2008–2009 school year to balance their strained budgets.
> - Because programs for gifted learners depend so heavily on local districts or states, they vary widely. It is common to have a district with special classes and services next to several others with nothing at all. After spending funds to raise achievement for their lowest achievers, poor urban and rural schools typically have nothing left for their most promising students.
> - Parents of gifted learners are fleeing the public schools as they realize that NCLB forces teachers to leave the high-ability students to their own devices and focus primarily on raising the achievement of struggling learners. This translates into little opportunity for gifted students to use higher-level thinking skills, to accelerate learning, or to explore creative or imaginative ideas.
> - According to leading experts in gifted education, the lack of a national commitment to gifted and talented children will not only prove harmful to the students but to the country itself, as the years of neglect take their toll and the next generation of innovators cannot compete in the global economy.

## The Children Left Behind

The plight of advanced learners practically becomes a nonissue in the high-pressured environment of schools today. Teachers often notice students who finish their work quickly—the doodlers and daydreamers who are too few to warrant an overhaul of the curriculum but too potent of a presence to ignore. Many teachers enjoy these children. They pose interesting questions, offer new solutions, and love to expound on their many opinions. Eagerness surrounds them as they work. Over time, however, their energy dissipates as they slacken their pace, hold themselves back, and censor themselves to avoid the annoyed looks and sighs of peers. These children are *left behind*—behind their own ability and potential as learners—to the same degree as those who struggle to keep up with the academic demands of their grade.

Talented young mathematicians and writers cannot thrive in a school where teachers feel driven to bring all students to grade-level proficiency by 2014, a priority that often translates into basic and often slow, lockstep lessons. In "education as horse race" (in this case, the race to minimum proficiency), learning focuses more on the finish line than the journey. Advanced learners—especially the creative, spirited, and independent ones—care more for the journey. The unforeseen discovery, the hot pursuit of new knowledge, the testing of a novel idea transport them from the small world of the textbook to a vast universe they can see, feel, and understand. Because gifted students do well in the horse race, their problems may appear nonexistent to the school. Who would guess that a child who makes excellent grades and knows most of the year's curriculum is actually at risk of underachievement? Such an idea seems counterintuitive.

The failure of our most promising youth is a quiet tragedy. E. Paul Torrance (1980) gives us the sad example of Tammy Debbins, a gifted first grader from the projects with an IQ of 177 who had an imaginary friend. The school didn't understand Tammy's needs and couldn't provide the kind of adjustments that would have developed her abilities. By third grade, Tammy's academic performance had become average. Torrance reported that she never used her talents in later years and that her greatest frustration in life was that she wasn't "very smart" (p. 152).

Underachievement is underachievement, whether it's a student treading water in the standard curriculum or a student getting straight A's. Without understanding that these learners need more than the standard curriculum to grow and develop, most districts fail to support teachers' efforts to accommodate them. This next teacher told us her story:

> My superintendent does not believe in segregating students by ability levels. So advanced students are doomed to sit in a class mix with all levels and all behaviors. As my district gains more low-level special needs students, the higher-level kids have begun to lose their motivation to stretch themselves and seek enrichment. For years, I have fought the case that gifted students need to be ability grouped with, at the very minimum, students of average ability. I finally won my argument, and this year I have one class of students whose standardized scores placed them in the above-average range. The change in their motivation is startling. I have created a challenging program for them and eliminated what they consider the boring, repetitious work. I must assume they can and will independently read conceptual material and can devote class time to enriching and fun labs and activities. I have told them, in no uncertain terms, that I will not accept mediocre from them in my class. To date, I have seen positive outcomes.

We have to consider what a life of easy achievement does to students over the long haul. They become used to collecting A's like prizes they can win with minimal effort; they begin to disengage from school as a place to learn. Others, like Tammy Debbins, lose sight of their gifts and slide into a life of underachievement and invisibility. They achieve as far below their ability as any other student targeted by the NCLB Act.

---

### What are your greatest challenges?

What makes supporting advanced learners difficult for you?

What services does your school offer?

What resources does your school offer?

What is the attitude toward these kids in your community?

How are your advanced students doing?

What would you like to do for them if you could?

---

## THE ADVANCED STUDENTS IN YOUR CLASSROOM

Many teachers can easily spot advanced learners through academic performance and test scores. Yet high ability does not always show itself so clearly. A student might have an unstable home environment that distracts her from attending and participating in class, or she might be a child who simply does not test well. One helpful way to expand our understanding of whom the advanced students are in our classrooms is to explore their thinking, learning, and behavior patterns in three broad categories:

1. Advanced intellectual ability

2. High degree of creativity

3. Heightened sensibilities

In this book, we use the term "advanced" rather than "gifted" to include the many students who can demonstrate their need for greater academic challenge, but who may not be formally identified as gifted.

### 1. Intellectual Ability

Intellectual ability includes academic aptitude—talent in areas emphasized in school, such as language arts, math, science, and social studies. More broad, intellectual ability also embraces a range of skills and thinking processes that some may consider less intellectual such as intuition, experimentation, instinct, or inspiration. Academically able children can absorb, synthesize, and analyze information easily. They may be advanced readers with precise and detailed memories, able to digest new concepts quickly, comprehend meaning and application, and use logic and critical thinking in complex ways. Yet these academic gifts often accompany a deep curiosity about many things, a need to question and challenge convention, and a desire to know why certain phenomena are as they are. When you think of intellectual ability, think about the *whole person*.

---

### How do your students show intellectual ability?

- Prefer to work and play independently
- Can multitask—concentrate on two or three activities simultaneously
- Prefer the company of older kids and adults to that of children their age
- Read books and magazines intended for older kids and adults
- Show interest in cause-and-effect relationships
- Want to know the reasons for rules—and the reasons *behind* the reasons
- Learn quickly and apply knowledge easily
- Show an unusual grasp of logic
- Have an advanced vocabulary for their age
- Love math games, playing with number concepts, and figuring out how to solve math problems in unique ways
- Seem extremely precocious—talk or think like an adult
- Show asynchronous (uneven) development—may be highly precocious cognitively while demonstrating age-appropriate or even delayed development emotionally or socially
- Love to know and give reasons for everything
- Argue or debate about the logic of ideas, rules, or actions

---

## 2. Creativity

Educators and parents have long seen creativity in their children. However, creative ability is difficult to measure. In schools that rely on standardized tests to identify advanced learners for special programs, the imaginative student with a quirky sense of humor may not qualify. Creative children apply logic to problems, explore solutions, and synthesize relevant information. Where they differ is in the creative way they do all these things.

Creative thinkers tend to push logic to its limits. Instead of saying, "If this is so, then this must also be so," they say, "If this rule applies here, can it also apply to this other situation? Can I adjust it to make it work? If not, why not?" They feel an inner impulse to look for what's new and unfamiliar.

You might find their school papers framed in clever doodles. Faces of imaginary beings peer out from the corners. Some creative kids are day-dreamers who find it difficult to stay on the beaten path. They always want to know what mysteries lie in wait for them around the corner, up the next hill, or beyond the horizon.

---

### How do your students show creative ability?

- Discuss or elaborate on ideas in unusual ways
- See many possible answers to questions or solutions to problems
- Are extremely curious, ask many questions, and question the answers
- Enjoy making discoveries independently and solving problems in their own way
- Like to play with words (rap, poems, jingles)
- Have a long attention span for things that interest them
- Become so involved that they're not aware of anything else
- Have many unusual hobbies or interests
- Have elaborate collections and are passionate about them
- Have a vivid imagination
- Invent games, toys, and other devices
- Think of new ways to do things
- Like to create by drawing, painting, writing, building, experimenting, storytelling, or inventing
- Enjoy singing, playing an instrument, dancing or moving rhythmically, or pantomime
- Respond to music, are able to improvise tunes and rhythms, or compose songs
- See patterns and connections that others don't see, even among things that appear unrelated
- Tend to rebel against what's routine or predictable

---

## 3. Sensibilities

When advanced students are learning, they connect to the process in a deep, internal way, absorbing the world through every pore. Life provides them with multiple and complex sensations. They may be stopped cold by the sight of Canada geese flying south at dusk, overwhelmed by the pounding beat from a passing car radio, energized by blowing leaves, or fascinated by a thunderstorm. They're often acutely attune to their senses—the feel of mud squishing through their toes, the spicy smell of baking gingerbread, the warmth of a fire near cold feet. While most children respond to sights, sounds, smells, and sensations, gifted children tend to feel everything in more depth and detail. Their impressions often stay with them a long time.

High-ability children may also show their gifts through empathetic responses to other people's struggles. They feel the sadness or distress of family members, relatives, or friends, and they recognize the fear of a dog who feels threatened. They offer friendship to an ostracized classmate or defend a bird trapped in a vestibule from the harassment of less sensitive children. Advanced students also tend to ask many questions about world problems—poverty, war, or pollution—and express genuine concern for the victims of injustice or hardship.

## Do any of your students seem overly intense?

### Overexcitabilities

Polish psychologist Kazimierz Dabrowski (1902–1980) identified five domains of what he called "overexcitabilities" or "supersensitivities," which he concluded were *inborn* and resulted from a heightened ability to respond to stimuli. They are the following: psychomotor, sensual, intellectual, imaginational, and emotional. Most commonly found in gifted and creative people, these overexcitabilities do not represent quirks of character but express much deeper qualities in the way they sense, experience, and process life around them (Lind, 2001).

The primary sign of this intensity in the emotional domain is an exceptional sensitivity to everything around them, a depth of feeling they try to mask but can rarely control. For these students, all senses seem to be amped up to a high level, and their emotions come into play whether they're relishing an interesting math problem or watching a lunar eclipse. In today's climate of facile diagnoses, they may look like children with emotional disorders. Their daily experiences invoke a wider spectrum of feelings that they find overwhelming at times.

Think about your students. Do any of these characteristics sound like them?

- Intense emotional extremes
- High sense of drama around minor events
- Heightened sense of responsibility
- Concern for others
- Feelings of being overwhelmed, inadequate to deal with large problems
- Strong sense right and wrong, of injustice and hypocrisy
- Detailed memory for feelings
- Timidity and shyness
- Loneliness
- Problems adjusting to change
- Struggles with depression
- Need for security
- Physical response to emotions

See also the following:

Daniels, S., & Piechowski, M. M. (2009). *Living with intensity: Understanding the sensitivity, excitability and emotional development of gifted children, adolescents and adults.* Scottsdale, AZ: Great Potential Press.

Another sensitivity commonly found in advanced learners is intuition—an insightfulness that enables them to see and feel things beyond their years, to read a person or situation beyond the surface appearance. That same intuitive ability enables them to work through a math problem or science project in a new way. An insight simply comes without any conscious reasoning process. Intuitive people suddenly sense something they can't explain logically. A child might say, "I don't know how I figured this out. I just had a feeling it would work."

For many advanced students, the downside of emotional sensitivity is perfectionism. Accustomed to excelling at many things and receiving praise for their accomplishments, they feel pressured to reach higher peaks with each endeavor. Unaddressed, this problem is a thief, robbing students of the joy they once felt in learning for its own sake. Perfectionists often put off starting projects because they can't bear to attempt what they can't do perfectly. The freedom and energy that once inspired their pursuit of knowledge gradually give way to stress about how they appear to others.

---

### How do your students show their supersensitivities?

- Show fair leadership in organizing games and activities and in resolving disputes
- Have a well-developed sense of humor and use it to ease tensions and bring joy
- Tune into the speech patterns, behaviorisms, and vocabulary of different people and imitate them with uncanny precision
- Are very active, have trouble sitting still
- Like to discuss philosophical ideas such as the nature of creation, love, justice, and equality
- Express unusual sensitivity to what is seen, heard, touched, tasted, and smelled
- Show sensitivity to the feelings of others and empathy in response to others' troubles
- Express concern about world problems such as endangered animals, racism, pollution, and poverty
- Show a willingness to follow intuitive hunches even if they can't immediately be justified
- Demonstrate high energy, focus, and intensity
- Are frustrated by imperfection in others and in themselves
- Are extra sensitive to criticism
- Show intuitive sensitivity to spiritual values and concepts

---

## Factors That Affect Advanced Learners

The popular profile of smart students—quiet, studious, and alone, with their noses in a book most of the time—may hold true for some. But apart from the differences in learning style or inclination that might make one child an incessant builder and another writer, other factors influence the way advanced children behave and function in the classroom. Consider the following as you observe your students:

*Disabilities.* A physical, emotional, or learning disability may overshadow an otherwise highly able child. It's common for a student to be twice exceptional—to have both exceptional gifts and a disability. When this is the case, schools often focus on the disability, leaving the young person's exceptional abilities unnoticed and unchallenged.

*Age.* Though a number of schools provide services for gifted students, rarely do they offer them before the third grade. Yet advanced learners—whether identified as gifted—have as much of a need for growth and challenge in the younger grades as in the later ones. A second grader who reads a middle school novel or a third grader studying aerodynamics on his own is most likely learning below his potential. Without any opportunities to use these talents in school, students can become detached or apathetic about learning early in life.

*Gender.* Gifted girls and boys face unique challenges in school. Social stereotypes about gender seep into peer relations from the first day of class. Kids with acute observation and understanding pick up the cues and expectations that tell them what is or isn't "cool" behavior. A gifted girl may censor her voice or camouflage her ability because she doesn't want to draw attention to herself; few girls in her class demonstrate much interest or ability in math or science, both subjects she loves. Gifted boys suffer similar pressures to conform—particularly if they want to pursue talents in subjects considered unmasculine, such as the arts or poetry.

*Culture.* Highly able students from minority, bilingual, or other cultural backgrounds face unique obstacles to their development. For example, many children from other countries have to deal with family pressures to pursue careers in specific fields—such as business or medicine—and this may cause them to avoid subjects they secretly love. A child who speaks another language at home may not be proficient in English, and thus her difficulties with reading and writing may mask her true verbal and analytical abilities.

*Family stresses.* Economic, work, and family pressures can make sensitive gifted children preoccupied with worries outside of the school. Even in relatively supportive homes, students might have practical problems that distract them from their work: a lack of space for study; a noisy, cramped living environment; or the daily pressure to care for other children. From these circumstances, they perform significantly below their ability.

Without knowing about the family and culture at all, teachers can easily overlook these diamonds in the rough.

## Practical Ways to Assess Advanced Learners

Knowing your advanced students' abilities and level of skill and knowledge doesn't have to involve a long assessment process. Always do what is reasonable given your time constraints and the specific information you need. Part of assessment is to realize how much you already see and know. A quote by Charles Peguy is apt here: "One must always tell what one sees. Above all, which is more difficult, one must always see what one sees" (Peguy quoted in Smutny & von Fremd, 2010, p. 35). To best serve the students in your class, turn first to the essential concepts and skills you'll be introducing in a subject and then explore where their strengths, abilities, experiences, and interests lie.

*Observe.* You begin with observation, something already ingrained in your daily life as a teacher. The checklists in this chapter provide a starting point for noticing specific indicators of ability in your students. Divided into three domains (intellectual, creative, emotional), the lists may also remind you of past events and sharpen your observation of specific traits that seemed insignificant before. Who are advanced learners? How do we find them? Though some teachers rely on test scores to identify exceptional ability, testing rarely goes far enough. You might have a reclusive young child in the corner who doesn't test well but who writes science-fiction stories, using principles of physics that she's learned in a workshop. A teacher once told of a five-year-old child named Mario who read more into test questions than his peers did. When asked what the color of coal is, he checked all three choices: black, purple, and gray. When questioned about his response, Mario replied, "It's black when I see it inside, it's purple when I see it in the sun, and after it's burned it's gray." (Smutny, Walker, & Meckstroth, 1997, p. 124).

*Use multiple criteria.* The use of *multiple criteria*—different venues and media for children to show what they can do—provide more ways for you to assess student behavior, thinking, social relations, emotional maturity, assignments, and so forth. Observing them respond to a broader spectrum of learning experiences leads to a more complete picture. A map project, a poem, a reenactment of a famous political debate, a research report, and a three-dimensional geometry experiment are ideal contexts for probing their interests, thinking strategies, and creative ideas. What does all this data tell you about their learning needs in the current unit?

Assessment ensures that you have the information you need to determine (a) how prepared the students are for the work at hand; (b) what skills, knowledge, and abilities they bring to a new unit or lesson; and (c) what adjustments may be necessary to ensure that they advance at their pace and level. Quizzes and tests have their usefulness in establishing a child's level of mastery as well as in identifying potential problems. But the strategies in the following chart widen the lens considerably and provide more information for you to draw on as you design alternative learning experiences for advanced students.

| Informal Consultations | Direct Observations | Portfolios and Anecdotes | Charts and Checklists |
|---|---|---|---|
| • Parent consultation<br>• Teacher-child conversations<br>• Peer sharing | • Main teacher<br>• Resource teachers and aides<br>• Parents | • Student work<br>• Anecdotal records<br>• Notes and grades | • Checklists<br>• K-W-L charts<br>• Rubrics |

*Preassess.* When beginning a new unit, you need to know how much of the content your advanced students already know, what skills they have, and where the gaps in knowledge and conceptual understanding are. Without this information, it's difficult to gauge their progress or know if you're meeting their needs. Your preassessments can cover a significant portion of a whole unit, include critical and creative thinking, and/or target specific skills you want students to master.

Preassessment not only tells you where children are in their understanding but brings their prior knowledge to bear on a new lesson. It can be motivating for students to realize, "Oh, I already know some things about this!" Many teachers use K-W-L charts (Ogle, 1986) where students describe what they *know* about a particular topic, what they *want* to know, and what they *learned.* The chart becomes a building block to a new learning experience. After they've participated in class, practiced a skill, or applied a newly learned process, they return to their list of what they know; they then make corrections where they see them and review what they want to learn to see if they've found the answers to their questions. There are other options besides K-W-L charts, but we mention them here because they're simple to use and apply to the immediate learning goals in your unit.

Starting a new endeavor is always the hardest part. It often seems to be a lot of trouble, with too little time or support. Why would we do this? With respect to advanced students, the answer can only be because it is the most humane thing to do. And being humane surely must rank among the most important qualities of any educational system. Without any intervention, advanced learners live like caged birds, imprisoned by attitudes, policies, and practices that won't allow them to be themselves. William Blake's statement, "No bird flies too high if he soars with his own wings," expresses the spirit of the chapters ahead and our desire to release the potential in every child. We hope you will enjoy the journey ahead!

## PARTING THOUGHTS FOR YOUR JOURNEY

*Begin simply.* If you care about advanced students, which you do if you're reading this book, then you probably have some grand schemes to implement. Break them down into small pieces. Start small!

*Observe, observe!* Don't rely too heavily on test scores, which can be misleading. Use the checklists as a guide and rely more on what students do and say, as well as how they express themselves.

*First things first.* Obviously, you have priorities as a teacher, and these are rarely of your making. Clarify how much of your time and resources they demand. Then, see if there's a way to provide more challenge for advanced learners while fulfilling other responsibilities. It need not be an either/or situation.

*Know their gifts.* As with all children, advanced students are also highly individual. They might have exceptional scores in mathematics but are also creative, relishing the chance to pursue unusual solutions. Become a keen observer of all the idiosyncrasies of your students—their interests, learning styles, work habits.

*Reach out.* We have heard too many stories of promising students coming to life because of the sympathetic ear of a teacher. As obvious as this may seem, it is a fact that small acts of kindness can be transforming moments. Giving a little time to a treasured interest of a child and affirming her ideas can break the isolation as nothing else can.

# Making the Most of Your Resources

*"As important as knowing what more I can learn and do is knowing how far I've come and what I have to give my students."*

—English-as-a-second-language (ESL) Teacher

When first introduced to the needs of advanced students, many teachers sigh over what they see as another demand on their busy lives. Children with special learning needs—whichever side of the spectrum they fall—can easily overwhelm a school district facing budget cuts and an overburdened staff. Questions immediately rise about time and resource commitments: Do teachers have to learn a completely new system? Where can they find new resources? How can they do this when they're already struggling to accommodate so many different needs in their classrooms?

The assumption here is that teachers have to go outside themselves to help advanced learners. But this is not always the case. Though locating new resources and materials for students is always beneficial, teachers can also find what they need *within* themselves—their experiences, networks, and resources. Just as students are not empty vessels to be filled, teachers are not empty dispensers of knowledge. The field of education has a deeper appreciation of how individual character, ability, disability, emotional life, culture, history, and so forth mediate the complexities of cognitive growth in children. Education has given less attention, though, to the differences between teachers and to the way their strengths, talents, interests, educational background, and preferred teaching practices express themselves in the classroom. What we have found in visiting teachers' rooms is that many already include elements that meet at least some of the needs advanced students have. So it is not a question of starting over, but of extending farther.

## WHAT ELEMENTS IN YOUR CLASSROOM CAN HELP YOU SUPPORT ADVANCED STUDENTS?

Whatever approach they use, teachers need to carefully think through what strategies will benefit their classrooms as a whole and how they can use them in a manageable way. Some adjustments are easier than others. Creating an alternative writing assignment requires little extra planning while moving students through an accelerated math curriculum demands considerably more. Whatever strategy you wish to implement, the first question to consider is, What elements do I already have in place? What am I doing to adjust and adapt to the needs of advanced students right now? Some teachers become so intent on applying a new system or program that they lose sight of their successes—the daily teaching practices, discoveries, and innovations that already support advanced learners. These can vary widely. For example, a math teacher may use an inductive reasoning process to help students develop formulas—an activity that he can adjust for children with more sophisticated math skills. Another teacher with an interest in entomology brings an unusual beetle specimen to class for students to investigate and report on. A teacher who experiments with collage assists students in composing original art pieces that combine their designs with free-verse poems they wrote in a language arts class.

So what can you, as a person and teacher, bring to your classroom that supports advanced students? This is an important question to ask. When we asked this question of Chicago-area teachers, this is what some of them wrote:

> "Although I'm required to follow the curriculum, I feel free to express myself a great deal in the classroom. I use a variety of teaching strategies to engage students, and let them make choices in how they want to convey what they've learned. Some activities have included poems, research papers, posters, mock websites, commercials, and radio jingles. When teaching food groups, I have taken my students to the

grocery store for a scavenger hunt. They've also made menus for a specific type of restaurant using all the food groups."

"I try to integrate music and creative writing on a regular basis. I'm looking for ways to integrate theater and dance at this school. At my last school, we did a unit on Shakespeare where this was easy to do. At my current school, we have extension units based in social studies and science where I'm hoping to integrate similar strategies."

"I'm a big fan of guided inquiry, discovery, and self-initiated research. Let's say we're taking a hike in the woods. "How can you tell one tree from another? Let's look for clues that might help us identify these trees." I always carry field guides for the children to delve into for more information. And this is the point: Always have resources at your fingertips so that a kid can get into the habit of looking things up, searching, and inquiring."

"As a musician, I've used music in the classroom, having students respond to the music they hear in different ways, as well as working with them on song parodies within different subjects, especially math. Theater is also engaging—another way to help students express themselves—a few props, a topic, and they take off!"

## What intelligences and learning styles draw you in?

Student learning styles have taken a more prominent place in education over the past decade. Howard Gardner's (1993) work on multiple intelligences (linguistic, musical, logical-mathematical, visual-spatial, bodily-kinesthetic, interpersonal, intrapersonal, and naturalist) has led more teachers to consider the ways their students learn best. The child who needs to build, experiment, dramatize, construct, manipulate, mime, and so forth is no longer doomed to spend her days on pen-and-paper tasks that she would tolerate better if she could only *do* something with them. A teacher is more likely to recognize the student who would rather experiment with several different strategies to solve a problem from the one who prefers a linear approach.

*Your* preferences as a teacher are just as important to this process. Which of these intelligences draws you in? Do you gravitate toward the bodily-kinesthetic domain, such as, constructing, building, moving, simulating, and the like? Or are you more at home with the written word—with speaking, reading, exploring metaphoric language, and playing with rhymes and rhythms? Awareness of your preferences can assist you in integrating them more into your daily teaching as a tool for supporting advanced learners. The more you broaden the ways you approach a topic, which means the materials you use to introduce it and the activities you design to engage students, the more analytical, creative, and inventive they become.

Besides the intelligences, there are other factors to consider, such as cognitive styles. Here are examples:

*Creative/Conforming.* For example, you tend to consider a wide range of alternatives before deciding how to respond to an assignment or new responsibility, or you feel more comfortable clarifying procedures and expectations to follow a process correctly.

*Whole to part/Part to whole.* For example, you're one of those conceptual people who has to know the big picture before examining the details, or you prefer the process of discovering the big picture through the details.

*Nonlinear/Linear.* For example, you prefer exploring a subject from different angles and through a variety of media sources, or you like the clarity of following a clear line of reasoning, a cause-and-effect sequence with a distinct beginning, middle, and end.

*Inductive/Deductive.* For example, you feel naturally drawn to situations where you can reason about the nature of a thing by examining many samples, or you would rather begin with a clear premise or base of knowledge and reach logical conclusions about each sample.

*Easily distracted/Long attention span.* For example, you feel enthused about many things and have to watch that you don't get distracted by other issues, topics, or interests, or you are highly focused, tune out everything but the task, and can delve into a topic with sustained attention and depth.

It can be helpful to do an inventory of what you bring to the learning table: your knowledge, teaching preferences, talents, experiences, and skills. The following chart is not comprehensive but intended as a catalyst for your reflection.

---

### Taking stock: What can you offer as a teacher?

**What personal qualities do you feel make you able to support advanced learners?**

**Examples**

- I like to be spontaneous even though I'm restricted by my daily responsibilities.
- I love creativity, though I'm not trained in the arts. I find a way to put this in wherever I can.
- I'm empathetic toward advanced kids; I see how they struggle to fit in.
- I'm open to suggestions from my students, provided they're reasonable.
- I have a questioning mind, which I think the advanced kids appreciate.

*(Continued)*

(Continued)

**Which intelligences and cognitive styles best describe you?**

**Examples**

- Linguistic
- Musical
- Logical-mathematical
- Visual-spatial
- Bodily-kinesthetic
- Interpersonal
- Intrapersonal
- Naturalist
- Creative/conforming
- Whole to part/part to whole
- Nonlinear/linear
- Inductive/deductive
- Easily distracted/long attention span

**What are you doing in your teaching now that lends itself to supporting advanced learners?**

**Examples**

- I use a range of texts of varying levels of difficulty.
- I have the kids analyze points of view in studying literature, history, and media.
- I use simulation and theater exercises to get kids to interpret situations and discuss them.
- I use math games to help kids think in different ways; I put advanced students together.
- I start each day with a quote and have kids write a response to it, which they share at the end of the day.
- I've designed extension projects, related to kids' interests, that involve them in more challenging and creative assignments.
- I'm involved in a joint ecology project between our class and a classroom in another state; the advanced kids in my class are paired with advanced kids in the other school.
- I keep files of writing prompts for gifted writers.

**What outside interests and talents can you share?**

**Examples**

- Experience in theater
- Interest in immigrant histories in America
- Debate club
- Experience on several archeological digs
- Cartooning background
- Thai cooking
- Poetry readings

Though most teachers try to incorporate their strengths and talents into their classrooms, this is not always easy in a high-pressured environment that values test results over less quantifiable evidence of student growth. Tunnel vision can easily take over, restricting the kind of feel-as-you-go experimentation that creative teachers use to develop new material for their students. A teacher's knowledge of blues music, for example, could become part of a unit on life at the end of the 19th century for African Americans in the Deep South. By becoming more aware of their knowledge, experience, and talent (beyond the classroom), teachers can more easily exploit any situation that presents itself in their day as an opportunity to learn something new.

Here is an example. A teacher who knows how to change a tire took his class outside to observe the process. He allowed students to assist in appropriate ways. The exercise enabled him to illustrate concepts involving force, weight, and so forth—showing them the difference between two different tools for removing the tire lugs (Why does a longer handle work better?). While using the jack to lift the car, he asked about the mechanics involved: Why is it so easy to lift the car with this contraption when even a strong human being could not do it? This seemingly mundane skill (changing a tire) became a fascinating lesson, particularly for the advanced thinkers who, the teacher said, returned to the classroom "supercharged."

Besides what you individually bring to the classroom, there are also the resources you have at your fingertips—both material and human. Let's look at each of them in turn.

## What resources do you have?

An annotated list of resources at the end of this book will assist you in expanding your curriculum for advanced learners. As teachers, you know that the right source materials—be they in the form of books, websites, or games—can bring together all the necessary elements for meaningful discovery to take place. Just as an example, here are some of the resources shared by several Illinois teachers in mathematics and language arts (see Resources for more information).

### Mathematics

*Ed Zaccarro's math books.* Ideal for advanced students, the Ed Zaccarro books focus on the importance of math in real situations such as investigations of math mistakes in news media or explorations of how much money a hybrid car can save its owner.

*Fractiles.* These wonderful magnetic tiles facilitate an intuitive grasp of spatial relationships and invite deeper explorations into the principles of symmetry, along with a visual art experience.

*The David Schwartz books.* The David Schwartz books are an immense support to advanced math students. *If You Made a Million, How Much Is a Million?* and *Millions to Measure* engage intermediate and middle school students in big ideas about numbers. Then there are two other reference books—a term that does little justice, as these are proven favorites for gifted learners. *G is for Googol* has thoroughly enchanted many advanced students by the alphabetic tally of mathematics concepts—everything from binary calculations and units of measurement to observable phenomena from tessellation to Fibonacci numbers. A science version of this is *Q is for Quark.*

*Christopher Freeman books.* Christopher Freeman, a sixth-grade math teacher (as well as enrichment teacher for elementary through high school gifted students), has shared his strategies for getting students to make discoveries in math. His *Nim: Variations and Strategies* engages students in critical and creative thinking, provides an application of arithmetic sequences, and enables students to generalize their strategies into one fundamental principle; by playing several variations on the game of Nim, they discover their winning strategies. *Drawing Stars and Building Polyhedra* are equally rewarding. Through drawing different kinds of stars, students discover their mathematical properties and formulate conjectures about continuous and overlapping stars. All activities meet four distinct National Council of Teachers of Mathematics (NCTM) standards.

### Language Arts

*Mike Venezia books.* Popular as research tools, Mike Venezia's books about famous artists, musicians, and politicians are highly informative and lively sources that engage advanced young readers through intriguing facts about world figures, samples of great artists' works, and kid-friendly cartoons that bring these individuals to life with all their idiosyncrasies.

*The Mysteries of Harris Burdick* (Portfolio Edition; Van Allsburg, 1996). This book makes reading and writing an adventure for all students because the author clearly designed both the images and text to ignite their imaginations. The book offers a tantalizing collection of mysteries that teachers can easily use as creative writing starters. The publisher also provides a teacher's guide for ideas on how to make adjustments for different age groups and abilities (http://www.hmhbooks.com/features/

thepolarexpress/tg/mysteriesofharris.shtml).The pictures and captions motivate students to write or tell their stories and provide endless variations depending on individual needs and interests.

*The Art of James Christensen: A Journey of the Imagination* (Christensen, 1996). This may seem an unusual source for teaching reading and writing, but a teacher has found it an inspiration for her students and her. She uses his work to develop close observation, to create a prewriting process for the imagination and to expose students to new ways of thinking. A quote she shared from the book:

> I think many of us view imagining as being lost in the clouds and not in touch with reality—and if it's passive or escapist, it can be—but the positive, active side of imagination has immense energy and potential. As soon as we step out of the rutted path of known solutions and begin to exercise active imagination, we are given the reward of understanding that we have a far greater range of possibilities than we had known before. (p. 16)

*English Companion Ning.* The English Companion Ning is an extraordinary site for English teachers, providing access to a professional community that they sometimes lack in their schools. Teachers explore and share books, lesson plans, and a wide variety of classroom topics via discussion forums, blog posts, and multimedia.

*ReadWriteThink.* This is another excellent site that offers educators, parents, and professionals high-quality practices in reading and language arts instruction. It provides among the best in *free* materials. Every lesson plan on ReadWriteThink has been aligned not only to the International Reading Association/National Council of Teachers of English (IRA/NCTE) standards for the English language arts but to individual state standards as well.

With increased access to the Internet, many teachers today have the world's resources at their fingertips. Though this does not replace books, games, art materials, dramatizations, and all the other means for connecting to ideas, it is a powerful tool for student research and inquiry. An example in Chapter 6 is a social studies teacher who uses a teacher-designed website to help her students connect to primary sources in the Library of Congress (see p. 109). Advanced learners can discover the difference between primary and secondary sources and acquire the thinking strategies of a historian by analyzing the images of original documents. Another website, The Futures Channel (http://www.thefutureschannel.com), provides multimedia content in mathematics, science, technology, and engineering that offers real-life situations to research the concepts learning in class.

Think for a moment about what you currently use and what other materials might better support your advanced students' need for greater intellectual and creative challenge. Visit the Resources section at the end of this book for new ideas. Consider Gardner's (1993) multiple intelligences as a guide for your search. Do you have children who come alive in a map-making process? Have you noticed that some advanced students seem most engaged when they can work with their peers on projects? Or do you see that the distracted and chronically disorganized student is also the one who writes a more creative essay?

---

### Taking stock: What material resources do you have?

**What aspects of your classroom environment support gifted students?**

**Examples**

- I have learning centers with materials and resources that provide more challenge for advanced learners.
- I have flexible seating arrangements depending on the activities of the day.
- I involve kids in contributing to classroom displays and exhibits.
- I have art on the walls.

**What resources in your room can you use for teaching gifted kids?**

**Examples**

- Internet connection, excellent websites, and software
- Learning centers based on intelligences, allowing different responses to units
- Nature exhibit that changes every season
- Large biography collection accumulated over the years

**What resources in your life?**

**Examples**

- Personal contact at The Field Museum
- Journalism background
- Video experience
- Connections to a wildlife rehab center

*What human resources do you have in your school, professional life, personal life, community?*

It can be difficult to find the time to ask someone for assistance or to explore the possibility of a partnership with another teacher, parent, or professional in the community. Some teachers prefer to work alone; others worry about the planning time required to communicate and coordinate their efforts. But teachers can benefit in many unanticipated ways when they reach out to the human resources around them, whether they be other teachers, community leaders, or parents. Collaborations open the mind to new ideas in a way that books or workshops do not. They also provide immediate feedback. A teacher we know reported that sharing ideas with other adults has become the primary means for her to grow professionally because these connections yield ideas she can immediately use in her classroom. For this teacher, talking with someone *in person* means that she can get specific questions answered about her circumstances and can better adapt new ideas to the needs of her students.

Teachers who reach out to families also find a wealth of support and assistance when they take the time to explain their goals for the class and encourage parents to get involved. The following report from a teacher shows the difference a parent can make:

> If I had one piece of advice to pass on to other teachers, it would be this: Ask parents to help. I never used to do this myself, but when a mother came to my classroom one day asking what I could do for her gifted child who was underchallenged, I almost pulled my hair out in front of her. I wasn't in the mood to pretend anything, so I told her how demanding things had become for teachers in the school because of cutbacks and having so many kids at different levels. Without batting an eye, she asked me if she could help, and without batting an eye, I said, "OK, yes!" I learned a few things from this partnership. First, parents are a resource. Yes, I know some can be unreasonable and difficult, but most are not, and many have talents and abilities to share. This mother came in several times a week to work with the more advanced kids in the class; she also helped with other groups including several struggling readers. She brought in supplies for an art project, shared her travel experiences as a photographer, and assisted in a science unit on insects—another interest of hers. Because of this experience, I actively look for resources among the families of my kids. I send out a newsletter when I can, notifying them of upcoming units and activities, and I make my needs known. I feel strongly that teachers today can't do it all by themselves, especially with all the different levels of kids they have in one room.

The home is a child's first classroom, and her parents or guardians are her first teachers. When the classroom teacher stays in touch with the home, student progress increases. This is particularly the case for advanced learners whose needs often go unattended. By partnering with the family, and especially, by sharing the responsibility for nurturing the child's gifts, teachers can experience fewer burdens on their time and resources.

A key solution to supporting advanced learners in a time of scarcity, therefore, is finding others with similar interests and concerns. Consider this list. Who can you turn to?

*Gifted education coordinator.* Usually hired by the district, this person coordinates programs, initiates services if they're not already in place, supervises teachers of gifted students, and evaluates programs and services.

*Director of special education.* Some schools assign responsibility for gifted programs and services to the director of special education. This person is concerned with all special education services—for children with learning differences, disabilities, and behavior concerns as well as high-ability students.

*Curriculum coordinator.* If your school or district has no gifted education coordinator, and if the director of special education has little or no responsibility for gifted students, you could turn to the curriculum coordinator for support or ideas.

*School psychologist.* The school psychologist can be a helpful advocate for teachers wanting to help gifted learners. In some cases, the psychologist can be crucial in providing evidence that a child needs a different kind of placement.

*Fellow teachers experienced in differentiation, acceleration, and enrichment for gifted.* Teachers who've attended special workshops or who've gained some experience working with advanced students in a mixed-ability classroom are an ideal resource. Many are willing to share what they've learned with interested colleagues and may be open to collaborating on projects that benefit able learners.

*Parents willing to assist with gifted students:* Some teachers are nervous about involving parents. They get a bad rap at times, just as teachers do in some parent circles. However, teachers should consider that welcoming the talents of suitable parent volunteers is the surest way to extend learning opportunities in the classroom. Parents can often lead small groups, teach new skills and concepts, or assist in larger projects, to name a few examples.

*Community volunteers:* This could include retirees with special areas of talent they would enjoy sharing (chess, debate, physics, architecture, sculpture, etc.), educational volunteers from ecology centers, any individuals associated with the school, or friends of the school who are able to donate a few hours a month in enrich the classroom.

*Resource people in personal acquaintance.* Mining your personal connections can often help build a network of potential assistants. Anyone who has any expertise or talent that could expand a project or unit for advanced students is worth approaching. We've found that many adult professionals enjoy working with these children because of their enthusiasm, quickness, and independence. These individuals could potentially help with a class activity or offer themselves as mentors to one or two students whose interests match their own.

As you can see, you need not work alone. Supporting advanced students must be a shared responsibility, at least part of the time. Some teachers have said that finding people in their school is difficult, that, as one teacher put it, "collaboration is a rare bird." It takes time to find the right people. However, this same teacher did discover genuine willingness and interest in two seventh-grade teachers who collaborated with her in producing *Romeo and Juliet.* The project benefited her as an arts instructor and enriched the literature classes of the seventh-grade students who gained much deeper insight into Shakespearean language and drama than they would have otherwise. As you approach people in your school, community, and other spheres of your life, be open about the projects and topics you are planning for your classroom, and ask if they have any connections. Do they know anyone who would work with advanced students on an earth science project? Do they know any authors who might enjoy sharing their creative process with a group of talented young writers? By expanding your search, you stand a better chance of finding the helpers you need.

---

### Taking Stock: What human resources do you have in your professional and personal life?

**Who in the school could assist you in supporting advanced students?**

**Examples**

- Curriculum coordinator
- Assistant principal who's very supportive of advanced students
- Seventh-grade science teacher who has a science club
- School psychologist

*(Continued)*

(Continued)

**How can parents contribute to the lives of advanced learners in your room?**

**Examples**

- The parent group is willing to explore how they can help teachers with advanced students.
- A parent historian can assist in teaching about primary and secondary sources.
- A parent engineer wants to show how mathematics helps engineers; he has an idea for an activity on building bridges.
- Parents can provide useful information on kids' abilities and learning needs.

**What community members can contribute to the lives of advanced learners in your room?**

**Examples**

- Art teacher from community outreach studio
- Computer company executive from the neighborhood
- Alderman
- City "green" project coordinator
- Neighborhood newspaper reporter

**Who else can contribute to the lives of advanced learners in your room?**

**Examples**

- Online mentors, for example, who work with girls who have special talent in technology
- Partnership with another school in the United States or abroad

## HOW CAN YOU ADVOCATE FOR YOUR ADVANCED STUDENTS?

The dictionary defines an advocate (n.d.) as one that pleads the cause of another and one that defends or maintains a cause. As an observant teacher, you've probably noticed your students' abilities—their insightful comments and expressions of creativity, artistry, leadership, and empathy. You've encouraged these students with your enthusiasm, your search for resources to feed their curiosity, and your involvement in their joys and triumphs. Who, then, is better equipped than you to advocate—to plead, defend, or maintain—the cause of your gifted students? More to the point, who will do so if you do not?

Advocacy always begins with knowing the students well. This can take the form of evaluating assignments and test results as well as reaching out to families and community members. But ideally, it should also involve close observation of behavior (as described in Chapter 1) and opportunities for students to share their lives—what they have learned and experienced beyond the classroom, and what they most love. By welcoming other interests and talents, teachers discover much more about their students. Their stories, poems, specimens, experiments, paintings, drawings, and other products become a part of the classroom environment. For advanced learners, who so often feel disconnected, this act of inclusion creates a sense of belonging. Had the gifted second grader, Tammy Debbins, Torrance (1980) wrote of found a place for herself and her imaginary friend she chose to take around with her, she would not have slipped so precipitously from exceptional to average achievement.

Advocacy involves a more active response to the unique learning needs, abilities, and emotional challenges of advanced students. The following chart offers some suggestions.

---

### Advocating for Advanced Students

- Point out, in private, their strengths, talents, and abilities. Highly able students often feel invisible and some, like Tammy Debbins (Torrance, 1980), are invisible even to themselves.
- Show that you value them *as individuals*, not just for what they can do, as impressive as this may be.
- Encourage them to follow what they love as well as what they excel in.
- Question their choices, challenge their thinking, point out other options, inspire them to extend and expand their ideas.
- Help them take risks and feel comfortable with setbacks and mistakes. Celebrate boldness!
- Group them together on class projects so that they can learn from one another and feel less isolated from peers.
- Do whatever you can to give them appropriate challenges, whether this means giving them more choices in assigned work, arranging for them to study a subject at a higher grade, or helping their families find extracurricular programs or workshops.

---

Advanced students often know what interests them, where they feel held back, and what they'd like to do. Most would love nothing more than even a moment of conversation with someone interested in their ideas or a little encouragement during a time of self-doubt. It's easy to underestimate the power of simple acts of kindness. Some may argue that they do not go far enough in providing real solutions for the thousands of underserved students sitting in our schools. At the same time, encouragement in a child's talents and interests is often remembered years later. Many accomplished individuals can quickly name the people who stood by them when they were most unsure of themselves and when they felt vulnerable and doubted the worth of their ideas. This is advocacy. As a teacher who cares about advanced students, you've already embraced this role in your own way. Since this chapter focuses on making the most of your resources, it's worth highlighting a quality that demands so little time but gives so much to a struggling child.

## The Human Connection

We wanted to end this chapter with an example of what can happen when a teacher reaches out to an isolated child. The human connection makes a profound difference in the emotional well-being of advanced learners, especially in their ability to become more resilient in pursuing what they love and feeling as part of the world. Few escape the struggle of the social outsider. Junior high music teacher Jane Artabasy helped a gifted student whose struggle with the rites of connection brought great anguish. These are her words:

*I especially recall one steamy day of rehearsal in June, a few days before our final show of the year. A cruel taunt, whispered during a dance sequence, ignited a temper tantrum from one of my more volatile eighth-grade boys. (Let's call him Tim, a very gifted and talented loner.) Extended and foul-mouthed shouting ensued but, fortunately, no physical fallout. It was the end of the period, so I kept Tim after class. He had retreated to a corner of the room and hunched down over a desk. He glared my way, raised his palm, and yelled, "Save it! Whatever you want, Mrs. A., just forget it. I've heard it all, and I'm not interested. Everybody in this #@%^& place hates me, and I hate them. And this stupid school too. So just leave me alone."*

*One of my strong suits as a teacher was a hefty head of steam in a tight pinch and plenty of hot air. But this time, I resisted my preachy tendencies. The moment needed silence. Suddenly, the glare softened, and tears started streaming down Tim's face. He began sobbing uncontrollably. A wrenching sadness welled in his eyes, pouring out of him from that place in all of us where we bury our most secret pain. The hurt of many years, the anguish of being on the outside looking in, came rushing out of that boy in torrents of anger, frustration, and hopelessness.*

*It was not a moment for platitudes or tiresome bromides, and frankly, it didn't matter. A broken heart craves compassion, not expertise or technique. I spoke as quietly and gently as I could:*

*"Tim, all that may be true. I wouldn't claim to know what you've been going through. But I do know I don't hate you. In fact, I like you . . . very much. You're an incredibly good and sensitive person, and I'm so grateful to know you and to have you in my class." I paused. "You do belong here, on this Earth and in this room, you know, or you wouldn't be here. You just have to learn how not to be so hard on yourself."*

> *Our discussion took a few more moments and a few more turns. Then, at some point, he allowed himself a sort of half smile.*
>> *"You aren't lying are you, just to make me feel better? You really like me?"*
>> *I nodded enthusiastically. "Of course, doofus!"*
>> *"Well," he grinned, "that's not what I really want, but it's better than nothing."*
>> *We middle school teachers know to interpret those words as more than faint praise. Such a charming and disarming specimen is the American teenager!*

(Smutny & von Fremd, 2009, pp. 15–16)

This touching example of advocacy gave Tim a place of his own in the classroom and the possibility of seeing himself through another's eyes. As Mrs. A. observed, "When perceived through our most creative impulses, the fabric of learning is a seamless garment, woven from the cloth of our whole selves" (Smutny & von Fremd, 2009, p. 13). This aspect of advocacy cannot be measured in data, nor can we know how far such an act of compassionate understanding can carry a student. What we do know, however, is that without this human connection, promising students have little courage to step into the world as freethinking people.

## PARTING THOUGHTS FOR YOUR JOURNEY

*Make the invisible visible.* Trying to support advanced students in schools or districts that seem to care little for their welfare can be over-whelming. It will help you if you can write a list of the personal resources you can bring to a particular subject or unit. The deficiency mentality (not enough money, no help, no support for gifted, no interest, etc.) can so easily sap a teacher's best intentions. Here's an example of what we mean.

---

**Class:** History unit (fifth grade)

**Students:** Two advanced students who've already finished the reading and assigned essay need a greater challenge.

### My Resources

**Personal Strengths:** Creativity, love of biography, and theater experience

**Material Resources:** Biographical materials, websites for primary and secondary sources, and arts materials

**Human Resources:** Family members of students, librarian, fellow teacher, actor friend (for possible theater-related process)

**Emotional Support:** I'm sensitive to my students (I notice when they're struggling socially), I encourage risk taking in a safe way, and I work hard to create an atmosphere of acceptance and excitement in my classroom.

---

*Know when you need assistance.* Educating advanced learners is not something many teachers can undertake on their own, and no one should expect them to. There will be times when you can clearly see that a child requires more intervention, possibly a change in grade level or, at the very least, a much more advanced level for a specific subject. With time, you will see the areas where students need more than you can offer. In this case, your advocacy may take the form of seeking alternatives for your students, possibly networking with parents, school counselors, and other teachers. Real solutions for advanced learners often combine different approaches—acceleration at another grade level in math, enrichment opportunities in language arts, an independent study in science. Supporting advanced students often means clarifying for yourself what you can do with the resources you have now and what you cannot. Knowing your limits as a full-time classroom teacher may become the catalyst that brings new helpers to your doors.

# Creating Appropriate Goals for Advanced Students

**H**aving goals in mind for helping advanced learners realize their potential is by itself an impetus for change. For instance, just knowing that you want to give children more *choices* in assigned work starts your mind percolating:

Couldn't I give them a choice of several books for that essay on civil rights?

Instead of reviewing for the test (which they don't need), couldn't I pair my two top math students to select a problem from one of the websites I visit for new ideas?

In a similar vein, you may decide that independent learning is a valuable goal not only for your advanced students but for all. The more students can do for themselves, the more time you have on your hands to create different paths of learning within the curriculum. You consider strategies for students to practice organization skills to meet deadlines. You notice that Rhea has trouble pacing herself because she tends to be a perfectionist about each step in a process, or that David goes overboard in the number of sources he uses in a research project. And you ask yourself the following:

How can I best assist students in defining their goals and ensuring that they don't become distracted or bogged down in any part of the process?

How can I help students prioritize tasks and pace themselves in longer class assignments or projects?

Despite their differences, advanced students all have a particular set of needs that are fundamental to their growth and development. Teachers cannot ignore these needs if they wish to respond more to high-ability children and provide the kinds of learning experiences that engage and inspire them. The ten-point summary that follows is not by any means comprehensive, nor is it meant to be. We offer it as a working list for you to refer to as you examine the most pressing needs of your advanced students and develop your goals for meeting these needs.

## TEN-POINT SUMMARY FOR INCLUDING ADVANCED LEARNERS

1. *Allow choices.* Try to offer more than one choice for advanced students to show what they know and understand. They benefit from a flexible use of materials and approaches in the classroom (choices in what materials they use, what process they engage in, and what assignment/project they will complete).

   Here are some changes to consider:

   - From a *simpler* to a *more complex* source. Advanced students report on a more difficult book than their peers for a research project.
   - From a *factual* to a *conceptual* process. Instead of studying the facts of Mexican immigration, they examine the causes and history of border crossings.
   - From a *single* source to *multiple* sources. They use text, websites, blogs, visual images, and so forth.
   - From *convergent* to *divergent* thinking. They use their experience and skill to create as many different formulas and methods as they can invent to solve a challenging math problem.
   - From *academic* to *creative* process. In addition to an essay or paper, they express their learning through other media— poem, collage, podcast, and so on.

2. *Encourage goal setting.* Give advanced students opportunities to participate in setting alternative learning goals for themselves. One way to do this is by displaying the day or week's schedule in the classroom. A teacher we know found that some advanced learners need to be able to see and process in their mind the sequence of the day's activities; it makes a difference in the way they feel in the classroom. They are often the ones asking, "What's

next? What are we going to do today? Now what?" Displaying the schedule enables all students to own their responsibilities for the day and to monitor themselves when they undertake alternative assignments.

Whether considered gifted or not, all students need experience in setting goals *for themselves.* Research demonstrates that setting goals has a powerful effect on student confidence and achievement. Advanced learners who come to school overflowing with ideas and energy need to develop the skill to break long-term goals down into smaller, short-term goals that are within their reach. When students set smaller goals that lead to a larger achievement they care about, two things happen: (1) They can focus their energy and ability, which would otherwise become diffused, and (2) they can measure their progress in a tangible way that reinforces their sense of efficacy as learners. Perfectionism, a common affliction of high-ability students, becomes more difficult to address in students who lack experience in goal setting. Instead of, "I must write a perfect report," students learn to direct themselves to a more realistic goal: "I must fill out the K-W-L chart on the subject of my report; then, I must work with my teacher to create a source list for the research I need to do." (See Del Siegle's web page on goal setting at www .gifted.uconn.edu/siegle/SelfEfficacy/section8.html.)

3. *Determine prior knowledge.* Always find out what advanced children have mastered. Nothing is worse than twiddling thumbs over lessons already learned. Advanced students come into our rooms with abilities, experiences, and skills—much of which they either hide or lay aside. Give them credit for the knowledge and skill they possess, and help them create alternative goals. Avoid drill-and-practice assignments that can cause boredom and potential discipline problems. Keep them engaged with a process that challenges their thinking and includes their interests. Try to assess their knowledge level prior to a new unit by a variety of means:

   - K-W-L chart
   - Daily observation
   - Consultation with other teachers and parents
   - Portfolio of prior work submitted
   - Informal discussion with students

4. *Accommodate pace.* Accelerated learning should always be part of anything you do for an advanced child, but it takes different

forms. In exceptional cases, a gifted child may be best served by skipping a grade. In this case, you need to advocate for the student through the channels available to you. Other teachers, administrators, parents, and, of course, the child in question must be part of the decision-making process. Usually, however, advanced students in your classroom can accelerate in less-drastic ways. Acceleration includes a broad spectrum of options—from assigning more difficult texts or research questions for a report to forming and coordinating a cluster group of high-ability students with another teacher. Advanced learners often acquire new concepts and knowledge quickly. This is important to bear in mind even if they lack knowledge or skill in a topic. It's easy to assume that if all students begin at roughly the same level of understanding, they will remain so. In fact, some children learn very quickly, while the rest of the class requires more time to synthesize new concepts or information. It's important to respond to this quicker pace of learning by providing advanced students with more challenging and engaging assignments (again, the K-W-L chart can support this process). As future chapters will explore, strategies such as compacting, independent study, and even creative thinking activities enable these students to learn at an appropriate pace for them.

5. *Include creative teaching methods.* These students tend to be out-of-the-box learners, so they occasionally need alternative ways to process new concepts and information. As much as possible, try to adopt a more creative mind-set to everything you do in the classroom. Too often, talented teachers fail to exploit the full potential of creativity, believing that they lack the skills or expertise to do so. But creativity is not about paintbrushes and poems; it is a way of thinking and an attitude. Consider the following general principles:

- Point out the hidden, less traveled paths and warn against set patterns.
- Assign work that requires creative and imaginative thinking.
- Nurture boldness in vision and endeavor.
- Impart coping skills to deal with peer judgment, perfectionism, and frustration.
- Support students' trust in their creative powers.
- Give them opportunities to correct errors, refine visions, improve, and elaborate.
- Find venues for students to show, demonstrate, perform, or exhibit.

6. *Accommodate interests.* Allow advanced students to explore their interests as much as possible. Again, the K-W-L chart will help identify what they're curious about and hence what motivates them. As much as possible, follow this curiosity. This is not always easy or possible in a classroom setting, but any opportunity you have to draw on student interest will greatly aid their growth and learning. Terrell Bell, former U.S. Secretary of Education once said, "There are three important things to remember about education. The first one is motivation, the second is motivation, and the third is motivation" (Bell quoted in Ames, 1990, p. 409). E. Paul Torrance (1983) wrote a now famous piece called "The Importance of Falling in Love With 'Something'" in which he guides young people to follow the path that most calls to them, to resist the pressures of others, and to celebrate and enjoy their greatest strengths. Time for students to share their interests with you or the rest of the class is a worthy investment when you consider that student engagement propels authentic learning experiences. As a teacher, you play a critical role in not only encouraging student interests and linking them to the units you've planned but in helping them to discover new interests. Consider these possibilities:

   - Interest-based learning opportunities
   - Student interest inventories
   - Consultations with parents
   - Portfolios for any student work (from home or class) that *they* particularly value
   - Exhibiting or sharing of student interests (e.g., art works, performances, inventions, collections, experiments, writing, etc.)

7. *Promote peer relationships.* For advanced learners, working with peers is critical. Social and emotional difficulties noticeably diminish when they have opportunities to learn with intellectual peers. You can arrange this in a variety of ways, as these examples demonstrate:

   - Pair advanced students together to share their ideas/thinking process in an alternative assignment (a challenging math problem or a research plan for a social studies exhibit).
   - Group advanced students together in an activity where they need the stimulation of intellectual peers in (e.g., literature circle).

- Collaborate with another teacher of the same grade to combine advanced students in a cluster group; share responsibilities for the group.
- Arrange for a parent, community member, or personal acquaintance to mentor a small group of advanced learners in a project.

8. *Integrate technology.* The inclusion of technology is a powerful bridge from academics to the real world. The flexibility of the Internet provides rich and varied learning options for advanced students. Smart Boards, blogs, e-mails, iPods, software programs, and Internet searches are among the many means to enhance learning experiences. Technology gives students access to an extraordinary range of sources and learning opportunities that they might never discover otherwise. In today's world, electronic mentoring, for example, could enable a talented science student to find a researcher with expertise on the Kilauea volcano in Hawaii and read updates on the most recent findings. The Internet also provides ways for students to collaborate with peers from other states or countries who share their interests. Apart from a significant enhancement to their academic and creative lives, technology also helps advanced learners feel more connected with others, less alone and isolated. (For excellent guidance on integrating technology into the classroom in a rational and manageable way, see *From Now On: An Educational Technology Journal* at http://fno.org)

9. *Independent learning.* Whenever possible, give advanced students independent activities or projects that permit them to inquire into a topic more deeply. A student who wants to create an oral history of his extended family's migration from Bolivia to the United States should be able to do so. If a project such as this requires more planning and supervision than you can manage right now, you can scale it down. The student could interview his parents and grandparents, design a map of their travels, or write a story about their journey from Bolivia and what happened along the way. Independent learning only works when students have opportunities to practice and develop the skills they need. Independent learning options often include some of the following skills:

- Completing tasks without adult intervention for longer periods of time
- Quickly grasping the main points of an assignment

- Using different sources to find information for a project
- Sharing responsibility in a group and showing initiative and leadership
- Demonstrating persistence in a challenging task
- Exercising organization skills to meet deadlines
- Taking notes and recording sound or visual footage to aid recall
- Becoming more self-aware as a learner and able to build on personal strengths and aptitudes

10. *Encourage self-assessment.* By this, we do not mean engage students in lengthy evaluations. The point is to help them reflect on what they have learned. Even having students write a paragraph or list of what they took away from a lesson or unit helps them see their progress and own it. Advanced learners need this kind of visual record. Recognizing, for example, that comparing the motivations of two groups of people in a land dispute helped them understand the problem better is important. Becoming conscious of what they know and how they came to know it makes them more aware of their learning process. Three examples follow:

- *Anecdotal records.* Journals where students write responses to their learning experiences or recordings of their responses on audio or video. Example: In an independent study project, a student recorded her thoughts and feelings about how she was doing at each phase. She specifically focused on four questions her teacher posed:

  a. What parts of your work today are going well in your mind and why?

  b. What problems are you having and what do you think the difficulty is?

  c. What do you enjoy most?

  d. What do you enjoy least?

- *Criteria lists.* Having a list of criteria for a project helps students monitor their progress and not become distracted by other interests or spend too much time on one item. A criteria list for a project on the science of flight could include the following:

  a. My project draws on at least two books and two web sites.

  b. The model of a bird helps me to demonstrate what makes a bird aerodynamic so that I can show it to my teacher and the class.

c. My final project includes at least one of the da Vinci designs and shows both its strengths and weaknesses (i.e., what made it aerodynamic and what its limitations were as a flying machine).

d. My airplane design addresses the concepts of weight, lift, thrust, and drag, and it includes an explanation of why I think it would work as a flying machine.

- *Follow-up.* Advanced students need opportunities to reflect on their experiences and assess their progress. Questions can assist in identifying what they do well and where they may need more knowledge or skill. Here are some examples:

a. What did you enjoy doing the most? Why?

b. What do you think you did best? Why?

c. Is there anything you feel you could have done better? What would this be?

d. Was there anything you had trouble with because you didn't know how to do it? Could you explain this?

e. If you were starting this project again, what would you change? Why?

Focusing on these strategies enables you to integrate them into your teaching at times when they can most benefit your students and when your time and resources allow you to do so. Treat the ten-point summary as a toolbox you can carry with you into the classroom. You won't use *all* the tools or apply any to all learning situations. Like all students, the needs of advanced students shift continuously depending on what you're teaching and what they bring to the work. A fast learner may not always benefit from an accelerated lesson. A highly creative student needs to gather information and build skills. A child who loves to analyze and take apart math problems can't always do so if he lacks understanding of certain operating principles.

From the last chapter, you explored what you, as a teacher, bring to the classroom (i.e., the talents, resources, and expertise that you can draw on to meet the needs of advanced learners). You've designed your environment so that students can use the resources you've collected; you've pooled together a variety of materials and media to allow a wider range of

**What can you do?**

Can you

- allow more than one choice for fulfilling an assignment;
- adjust pace for those who learn more rapidly;
- include creative options for learning, studying, and applying new concepts;
- incorporate student interests; or
- group advanced learners together?

learning options; you've created stimulating catalysts for new units. You might even have a parent willing to assist or a friend whose particular talents could open a new world of exploration for your students.

A practical approach is to focus on those areas of the curriculum that are inherently *expandable*—where, with a little extra planning, you can allow more choices for those who need them. Guiding students to a more difficult book in either the classroom or library is an example. Helping them engage in this text through thinking questions and small-group discussion would extend the process further. Some teachers have also used Bloom's taxonomy to turn a relatively straightforward information-gathering process into a more analytical one. Others have relied on creative strategies to stimulate a more open thinking process or to encourage a different use of sources and materials. In every unit, there are moments when you can create new ways for advanced learners to use their talents.

Clearly, there is a range of responses to these students' needs and some involve more time than others. Giving children helpful suggestions on how to take their work to another level or guiding them toward a more challenging resource takes considerably less time than designing and supervising an independent study project. Between these two points, a broad spectrum of possibilities stretches out, limited only by your imagination.

For some teachers, structuring alternative learning opportunities for advanced students can become complicated by their tendency to do too much. Their imaginations carry them away. They realize too late that they have started something that will involve more time than they thought. Manageability becomes an increasing problem. You need to clarify for yourself—at the start—how much time you have and what sort of human and material resources you can bring to advanced learners. What is possible for you to do at this moment? What can you start doing now, and what should you put off for another time? What process or project might you be able to do in smaller steps or with the assistance of someone else?

---

### Making Change Manageable

**1. What can I do right now for my advanced kids?**

**Examples**

- Give Kira more difficult books and online websites to explore her report on the hooded chameleon.
- In a math class, use open-ended questioning for James to discover as many formulas as he can for solving a multistep math problem.
- Let Leah create a collage as part of her free-verse poetry poster.

*(Continued)*

(Continued)

**2. What do I need to support these kids more?**

**Examples**

- An assistant to work with a small group of accelerated students in my literacy class.
- An arrangement with the sixth-grade science teacher to allow an advanced student to participate in a science unit related to his interest.
- Strategies for how best to structure independent studies with advanced learners without having to spend too much time (I have other kids!).

**3. Where else can I turn for help?**

**Examples**

- Parents with special expertise in fields related to what we're studying (e.g., Jeremy's mother is an architect; Dana's father has a theater background).
- Community members who can assist in the classroom (e.g., Bilingual librarian; art teacher at the community art center).
- Other teachers who join me in a coordinated plan for advanced learners (e.g., music teacher to work with me on a history unit; math teacher to work with me on our "math explosion" problem-solving project).

The guiding principle in teaching advanced students is to follow their needs, abilities, and interests as much as possible. Though you undoubtedly have curriculum objectives and learning goals that you must adhere to, try to find any place where you can allow more variation and extension. Think of small changes you can introduce gradually in different subjects. If you want to try your hand at something that requires greater planning and supervision, do it in a unit you know well. In other words, avoid making the process harder by attempting large-scale changes in new units or by trying to do too much all at once, thus doubling the demand on your time and resources.

The course of action you choose will depend on three overriding concerns. Ask yourself the following:

1. What are the most pressing needs of my advanced students at this moment in time?

2. In which subjects are these needs most imperative?

3. What strategies might work best, given their particular needs and the subject at hand?

Keeping these three questions firmly in mind will bring focus to your planning and help you prioritize the needs you wish to address.

Here are some examples to help you think about your classroom.

| Subject Areas | Student Learning Needs | Examples of Strategies |
|---|---|---|
| Mathematics | • Need for faster pace when learning more advanced content<br>• Need for more difficult thinking problems<br>• Need for hands-on projects | • Curriculum compacting<br>• Inductive reasoning problems for kids to discover solutions<br>• Building a tetrahedron kite with straws and tissue paper |
| Writing | • Need for a wider range of resources for a report on a current event<br>• Need for creative outlet | • Guided inquiry for exploring websites with primary and secondary source materials<br>• Drawing, painting, or making a collage as a visual representation of written report |

As just mentioned, when trying a new strategy for advanced students, especially one that requires more planning, start in the places where you can expand what you're already doing. Where is it easiest for you to loosen the constraints on the pace students learn? On the materials they use? On the kind of thinking they do to produce their work? Integrate new ideas into your daily schedule as you go.

---

### Examples From the Classroom

**Strategies I can implement right now include the following:**

- Allow novels that are more challenging for advanced readers.
- Use different media to represent solar system (collage, movement, or display).
- Create two choices for a writing response to the study of the Civil War.

*(Continued)*

(Continued)

**Strategies I can expand on include the following:**

- Learning centers can have sources that are more challenging for advanced kids.
- Family biography project requires more research on historical and political background.
- Inductive reasoning process in math allows kids to think outside the box.

**Strategies I'd like to learn about or plan for include the following:**

- Compacting
- Independent study
- Tiered instruction

**What I need to try these strategies includes the following:**

- More information on how to design an alternative learning process once I've identified what skills or knowledge a child has mastered (and can therefore skip)
- Advice on how best to design student contracts
- Help from another teacher or mentor on how to plan the different tiers and supervise them in a unit or activity

All teachers have definite ideas on how best to introduce new material to their students. Bear in mind these three questions: What are the most pressing needs of my advanced students at this moment in time? In which subjects are these needs most imperative? What strategies might work best given their particular needs and the subject at hand? By thinking these questions through carefully, you will arrive at reasonable goals for addressing the needs of advanced learners in your classroom. Next is an example of how this might work in a fourth-grade history class.

### What do my advanced students need most?

**Grade:** Fourth graders (seven advanced students, with two identified as gifted)

**Needs:** Higher-level thinking and sources that are more challenging for in-depth inquiry

### What subject gives me the most latitude and resources to reach these students?

**Subject:** History—opportunities to explore process of constructing history (analysis of sources, point of view, interpretation, etc.)

**Resources:** There are many avenues—both online and on the ground—for students to explore and interpret primary (interviews, original writings, or artifacts) and secondary (books, articles, or web sites) sources.

### What strategies can I reasonably use, given my obligations to the rest of the class?

**Change thinking process:** From learning historic facts to *doing* historic research themselves. For example, in addition to what they've learned through reading about immigration on the web and in libraries, students interview a relative or older friend about their experiences as new immigrants, and then write a story about their interviewee.

**Change sources:** From exploration of history books and web sources to evaluation of the source materials themselves. For example, rather than report what they've learned, students examine questions of authenticity and accuracy. How can they determine if a source is reliable? What is a primary versus secondary source? What are the benefits and limitations of each?

**Tiered instruction:** In a unit on the immigrant experience through Ellis Island, one tier writes a short essay on the causes of immigration for a particular group and the nature of their experience coming to Ellis Island. Another tier examines each step in the process of immigrating through Ellis Island and compares it to the process used today. Drawing on first-hand stories from both periods, students write a position paper on the fairness of the process.

**Creative option:** Based on reading and research, students assume the identity of an immigrant from a specific country and write a series of journal entries detailing their experiences; they accompany their entries with artwork where appropriate.

## PARTING THOUGHTS FOR YOUR JOURNEY

*Find engaging sources.* Sources are more than materials. They are catalysts for thinking, discovering, and creating. Regarding sources in this way, teachers find themselves always looking for new materials and ideas that have the power to inspire, motivate, and excite curiosity. Those initial moments of engagement in learning can make a lesson take flight. With web technology growing rapidly, teachers with access to the Internet possess a range of resources that spreads across the globe. It's easy to be swept up in the enthusiasm for all the new applications, software, gimmicks, and toys.

Yet looking at a screen and clicking sites present limitations. Within certain parameters, the technology delivers on its potential for giving students access to otherwise unreachable sources. But students also need the kinesthetic domain of learning, whether it's the comfortable little nook in the classroom where they read, the pile of clips they touch and manipulate in a math game, the open notebook and pen waiting for their next poem, or the found objects they use for constructing models. Reading about nest building on the web is simply not the same as creating a display of actual nests (abandoned at the close of mating season). A wall of prints representing the work of Frida Kahlo can do more to inspire writing responses than text or web searches. Students of all levels need to touch the world they're studying, not simply surf through it.

*Focus on big ideas.* Much of the success that teachers have experienced in differentiated instruction has come from focusing on big ideas—essential questions, principles, or concepts that lie at the core of a discipline or unit. Teaching big ideas creates a more open learning environment for advanced students. Let us take science. Because of the pressure on classrooms to cover prescribed amounts of content by the end of the year, students sometimes end up learning more about science, but doing less of it. Wiggins and McTighe (2001) in their book *Understanding by Design* pose useful questions to bring teachers back to the fundamental concepts, processes, and skills at the core of their subjects. What competencies in science will prepare your students for a lifetime of study and discovery? What is science really about for a first grader, fourth grader, and so on? What big-picture processes are implied in the standards and curriculum for your grade, and how can you bring these out in a way that promotes greater growth in all your students, including your most advanced ones?

For example, a major part of science is *observation* and *data collection.* Science students need many opportunities to develop their observation skills—to distinguish between species, perceive differences in behavior, explore cause-and-effect relationships, and make tentative hypotheses.

This is an example from a teacher:

> I enjoy watching my kids sigh when I first introduce science to them, knowing that they think we'll just be going through the text and doing a few experiments. I ask them what they think scientists do, and we explore some of the most important activities of the discipline, such as observation. I then tell them that they're going to do a lot of careful observation in the class and I can tell they're thinking "ho-hum." Then, I immediately put them on an assignment. Some years, it's been cloud formations, and other years, it is animals. The kids have questions to think about as they make observations and try to puzzle out what they're seeing. One bright girl in my class spent a lot of time observing a group of sparrows picking over crumbs. She noticed that certain birds pecked others away and "hogged all the food" but that then they would let them eat later. She showed me her notes and a sketch of how the birds were clustered on the ground. Her data became significant as the class explored the subject of social organization in animal populations, and the term "pecking order" became more meaningful.

—Third-grade teacher

*Use/exploit open questioning.* This is a simple device, but it can open so many doors for advanced students. Open questions may have right answers but they do not dictate how students discover them. For example, adding four and four can only be eight. But if you ask more advanced primary students the different ways they can add two numbers to get eight, this is a more interesting question. In the same way, you can ask advanced kids to add double-digit numbers, the assignment being to find as many different ways to do it as they can. In so many situations in teaching, you can find opportunities for open questions that turn what could be a somewhat limited assignment (for a gifted student) into a much more dynamic one. Do math students always have to add double-digits numbers from right to left? How else could they do it?

Switching for a moment from math to writing, open questioning can also assist students who feel uninspired. You can use the K-W-L chart to discover what they most want to know. What is the question that their report will answer? What is the thing they most wish to learn and want their readers to understand? In an essay on famed racehorse Sea Biscuit, for example, a student decided that, for her, the most important question was, What choices in the treatment and training of the horse made it possible for him to overcome his abusive past and begin winning races? Having this question in front of her focused her writing and research in a powerful way.

For a creative student who feels constrained by the writing process, you may have to think of other options. Must they write their reports from beginning to end, for example? What might be the benefit of students writing the conclusion first? Some students, especially creative thinkers, enjoy composing backward because it anchors their writing process to imagine how the piece ends. In fact, this strategy is an effective writing exercise for students who have trouble staying focused on what they most want to say.

Whatever goals you choose to pursue, however small, your advanced students will benefit. As you become more practiced and flexible in designing different learning options, you'll find yourself making adjustments spontaneously. It will become second nature. But this can only happen if you allow new strategies to take hold in a workable way and make the process your own.

# Meeting the Needs of Advanced Students

*Strategies to Begin*

"**W**hat can I do right now to help high-ability learners?"

This question often rises in a seminar or workshop on teaching gifted and talented students. Teachers want to know if there's anything they can implement right away that won't require too much preparation or planning. Often, someone will say, "OK, OK, I can see that doing X will help these kids, but what if I don't have time for that now? What can I start doing tomorrow?" Looking back at Chapters 2 and 3, we can affirm that some goals for teaching advanced students do not demand as much preparation as others. They are more within reach of your current teaching schedule, requiring minor adjustments or extensions to the units you've planned. This chapter focuses on these adjustments.

Creating more choices for advanced students most often starts with the classroom itself—not only the design of the physical space and its resources but also the culture of learning and sense of community that evolve there. In the old days of straight rows and worksheets, all children labored over the same tasks and exercises, and they did so in classrooms dictated by fairly uniform and rigid traditions and practices. In contrast, teachers today orchestrate a wide variety of approaches to the curriculum, and they begin this process by making the classroom itself an engaging place to learn.

This sort of classroom is dynamic, continually adapting itself to new needs as they arise. Michael Thompson (2000) once commented that too many children sit in classrooms, locked in "a kind of Orwellian isolation," (p. 2) studying and repeating the same things. "Already," he said, "they have lost the world, and the educational instructions they obey lead them farther and farther from the world as the looming walls of the classroom close in" (p. 2). Advanced students long for the life beyond the "looming walls"—undiscovered life forms, mysterious problems that defy solution, and complex patterns just beyond their grasp. They long to connect to the world in more meaningful ways—applying a math process to a real-world situation, discovering a new organism through a microscope, using a multimedia exhibit to illuminate a short story.

## LOOKING AT THE CLASSROOM

Making the classroom a place where advanced students want to learn may take some initial time and thought, but such an environment makes it easier to respond to their daily needs. Teachers are masters at designing their classrooms, but do they give themselves the time to think about the qualities they wish to express? Are they so pressured to conform their rooms to the demands of the curriculum, the testing schedule in the district, and so forth that they give little thought to the daily living that will go on there? Do they give thought to the student who wants to be a bug specialist or the bilingual child who writes poems in Spanish? In a sense, a classroom is learning home, and like your home, you want it to support not just the practical demands but the qualities that nurture the spirit and inspire the mind.

Consider these three dimensions of the classroom:

---

**1. Physical space—What in the space itself matters most?**

*Visual stimulation* (art, posters, wall hangings, colors, and shapes)

*Learning centers* (topics, learning styles, interests, and themes)

*Displays and exhibits* (maps, science projects, and artwork)

*Seating arrangements* (whole class, small group, and independent work)

*Inviting nooks* (cushions and couch for quiet reading and thinking)

---

*(Continued)*

(Continued)

---

**2. Daily routines—What daily practices contribute to community and belonging?**

*Daily prompts* (quotes, jokes, puzzling questions, and unusual facts)

*Music* (favorite musicians, composers, and instruments from around the world)

*Student shares* (amazing story, personal passions, and "aha" moments)

*Student responsibilities* (clean-up, storage, room arrangement, and civility)

*Movement* (whole class to small group, extension activities, and independent work)

**3. Atmosphere—What communications and standards make students feel safe?**

*Expectations clear* (procedures explained and criteria written down)

*Engaging catalysts for new lessons* (real-world connections and creative activities)

*Encouragement and respect* (risk taking is celebrated and criticism is discouraged)

*Positive peer relationships* (kids grouped by interests/strengths and bullying outlawed)

*Parental input* (parent assistance and parent mentoring of advanced students)

---

Beginning with the classroom itself makes sense because a prepared space enables you to create adjustments more simply. This is particularly true if the students become part of the process by sharing their poems, discoveries, or experiments; by creating exhibits; and even by bringing in objects needed for a unit—an old hat for a costume, for instance, or bits of colored wire, egg cartons, or Popsicle sticks for a math class. An environment that has not only color, music, and design but also things the students have made or that they've shared from their lives outside the classroom helps to foster a sense of community and collaborative learning. An example demonstrates this:

Jorge was the neighborhood graffiti artist and he preferred entire walls to work on; but one day, he said he'd done a nice piece about his family tree on a large piece of wood. I told him to bring it in. Our class had created a museum of student creations, and each week we featured about five works. They could be art pieces made of anything, inventions either made or sketched (and explained by the student to the class), crafts, and so on. During down times, we would gather around the museum and have the creators share their pieces, and the kids always love this. In fact, they are really bummed if we don't have time to do it.

—Fourth-grade teacher

---

### What about your classroom?

How can you make your classroom more engaging for advanced learners?

How can you help all students feel more accepted/safe in relation to peers?

How can your environment empower your advanced learners to use their talents?
    What else can you do to bring more of your students' lives to the classroom (e.g., artworks, inventions, poems, raps, crafts, cultural traditions, photographs of great moments, and humorous stories)?
    Consider these questions about resources:

- Do the materials reflect the broad interests and learning styles of the students?
- Are they consistent with the students' advanced developmental level, experience, and knowledge?
- Do they prompt questions, inquiry, and a sense of wonder?
- Do the materials stimulate higher-level thinking in different subjects?
- Do they inspire divergent thinking and self-expression?
- Do they enhance research skills and knowledge?
- Do they enhance the growth of creativity?
- Do they embrace the qualities valued by advanced learners—beauty, form, shape, quality of material, level of craftsmanship, and ingenuity of design?

---

The openness and stimulation of the classroom make it possible for advanced students to relate to their subjects at a more in-depth level. From their earliest years of life, all children develop and learn in a relationship with their environment—the people in their lives, the nooks and crannies they've explored in their neighborhoods, the animals they've seen and cared for, and the books they've worn out and scribbled in. This active process continues throughout life. Learning is *relational*, and no one understands this better than the teachers who try to connect their students' interests and life experiences to the subjects they study through the year.

Yet there is more to this than a connection. A connection can be a handshake or a quick greeting while rushing to the grocery store. Unfortunately, sometimes we have to teach like this when tight schedules deny our students the time they need to make a new discovery their own. However, the kind of learning that most serves advanced students (and, in fact, all students) helps them relate to the topics they study. This is what E. Paul Torrance (1983) meant when he wrote "The Importance of Falling in Love With 'Something.'" In the course of engaging in new thought, activity, and skill, advanced learners stumble on something that really calls to them. They connect to it on a deeper level, gathering all the information they can find from books, Internet sources, movies, and so forth. Although we cannot make every subject enthralling to our students, we can create in our learning environments all the elements that lead to creative engagement: a variety of resources centered around real-world applications, displays or exhibits of student work focused on these applications, and creative catalysts for introducing new units that allow students to draw on their interests and preferred learning styles.

## Anchoring Changes to What You're Already Doing

In recent years, differentiated instruction has given teachers some useful concepts to plan for student needs—one of the most helpful being the focus on *content*, *process*, and *products*. This focus anchors any changes you make—big or small—in the work you're already doing in the classroom: the topic you're teaching, the activities you've planned, and the assigned work of your students. This is important, as one of the greatest hurdles to assisting advanced learners is the responsibility teachers have to the other students. "While I'm off meeting with the faster kids, who takes care of the others?" The answer is that you can do both through flexible planning. For instance, you ensure that a reading/writing process can support higher-level thinking (gifted students analyze primary and secondary sources for a report). You create a more challenging version of a math assignment (advanced primary students find three different ways to solve a problem). You group advanced learners together (students do a science experiment in pairs or groups).

Consider the questions in the table:

| Content | Process | Products |
|---|---|---|
| • Does the level and pace of content match their abilities?<br>• Do they perform well in interdisciplinary studies—relating a topic in one subject to a similar one in another?<br>• Do their interests relate to any of the content? | • What are their learning preferences? (Do they need to share with others? Are they visual learners? Do hands-on assignments work best?)<br>• Do they prefer math problems that invite inductive reasoning?<br>• Do they incline toward the creative? | • Are there ways they can expand their assignment to create more challenge (e.g., a comparison between two books rather than a book report)?<br>• Can they add another dimension to their assignment to show what they've learned (a map, a design, or an experiment)?<br>• Can they use other technologies? |

As brought out in the previous chapter, advanced students need choices. Examining content, process, and products helps to think simply about the kinds of choices you can provide at different points in your day. In practice, the three interrelate. Changing one often changes another. Students working on a more open-ended math problem will naturally use higher-level, creative thinking, which, in turn, will result in more unique solutions. The following pages highlight the areas where changes make the most sense.

## Choices in Pace and Level

Generally speaking, advanced students need adjustment in the *pace* and *level* at which they learn. In practical terms, this means that most of them crave moving faster (they are the ones tapping their feet, doodling on paper) and trying their hands at something harder. They are tired of easy! They want to be stumped, to pit their wits against a sticky problem. Adjusting pace and level can be as simple as providing more difficult materials (books, websites, or activities) related to what the rest of the class is doing or asking her to formulate a position on a current issue by comparing the opinions of two experts.

> ### What can you do to respond to the students who finish first and always seem to know the material you have planned for the week?
>
> - Can you challenge them by using other sources, particularly in the different technologies available today—websites, blogs, iPod recordings, software programs, electronic mentoring, and so forth?
> - Can you adjust an assignment to include other layers of complexity and to demand higher-level thinking strategies such as comparing, analyzing, and interpreting?
> - Can you advocate for him to attend a higher grade in a subject?
> - Can you find a parent or community person willing to assist advanced kids who need and want a faster pace?
> - Can you allow advanced students to work in pairs or in a small group to collaborate on an independent study project related to the unit at hand?

By making your classroom more flexible in the sources students use, the kind of thinking they do, and the pace at which they work, you're able to reach more than those formally identified as gifted. Although we have no statistics on how many talented learners underachieve in school, anecdotal evidence has shown us that opening a unit of study to include more difficult or creative choices benefits many more children in the classroom. A student who rarely excels in a language arts class may try her hands at a creative writing process because it's new and different or because she has a story she's always wanted to write. Creating a broader range of choices for advanced learners can motivate underachievers who've never felt inspired enough to apply themselves.

### Higher Levels of Thinking

No one can discuss levels of thinking in education without mentioning Benjamin Bloom's taxonomy. Revised in the 1990s to make it more relevant to 21st-century teachers and students, the new taxonomy produced some significant changes (Anderson & Krathwohl, 2001). Most notably, the categories themselves had become verbs, reflecting the process aspect of thinking. In addition, the *creating* category replaced the former *synthesis category*, revealing the high cognitive level of creative processes. Here is the revised taxonomy:

- *Remembering.* Retrieving, recognizing, and recalling knowledge from memory
- *Understanding.* Making meaning from information in oral, written, and graphic forms and through processes like classifying, summarizing, comparing, interpreting, inferring, and explaining
- *Applying.* Using a previously learned principle, idea, or concept in a new but relevant situation
- *Analyzing.* Taking a situation, material, or topic apart, determining how the constituent parts relate to one another, often with the intent to understand its overall structure, nature, or meaning
- *Evaluating.* Making judgments based on criteria and standards through comprehensive reviewing and critiquing
- *Creating.* Putting elements together to form a coherent or functional whole; exploring and reorganizing the elements into a new pattern or composition through such processes as divergent thinking, improvising, elaborating, and transforming

Teachers can use this revised taxonomy for any students who need a more challenging or creative assignment. In the planning *you are already doing* for the rest of the class, you can design a higher-level thinking process for your more advanced students. Consider different approaches. The following are four possible scenarios:

Scenario 1: All students work through the remembering and understanding stages of a new unit and then select at least one question/activity from another level.

Scenario 2: Most children work at the remembering and understanding levels while the advanced kids respond to assignments at the analyzing level.

Scenario 3: Some children do assignments at the remembering and understanding stages and then do an optional process at

---

**A *Doing* Taxonomy**

**Remember:** Describe the main bodies of fresh water in the United States.

**Understand:** Summarize the condition of our country's fresh water supplies.

**Apply:** Construct a theory on how key threats to fresh water supplies extend to ponds, lakes, and rivers where you live.

**Analyze:** Examine causes of pollution and fresh water declines and how these forces have affected people, communities, and environments.

**Evaluate:** Assess whether you think fresh water supplies can sustain the country if these trends continue.

**Create:** Compose an essay, poster, or poem, expressing your thoughts about fresh water in the United States.

the applying stage. More advanced students select questions or activities from one of the higher stages—applying, analyzing, evaluating, or creating.

Scenario 4: All students learn at the remembering and understanding levels. Those who finish an assignment before the deadline can choose activities at any of the higher levels.

Here are some examples of how you can make adjustments in pace and level:

---

### Low-Preparation Adjustment

#### *Change Sources Used*

- *Texts.* A novel instead of a story, a book rather than an article, multiple articles rather than one, Internet reports, and blogs
- *Technology.* New websites; software for specific subjects; podcast software (for students to create their own podcasts); video recorder; editing instruction for videography, podcasting, and the like; blogging; and online mentoring/learning
- *Hands-on materials.* Construction materials for math concepts; arts supplies; samples of plant life, rocks, microscopes, and dead insects for study and analysis; costumes; props; instruments for measuring, weighing, and calculating; and notebooks for recording findings

#### *Change Thinking Process*

- From learning a concept to *applying* it to a new context: Students understand the difference between primary and secondary sources, and apply this to the kinds of sources they should consider for a report on a topic.
- From applying a rule or principle in one context to *comparing* how it works in two or more: Students learn the basic rule of the game of Nim by playing one game; then, through observation, repeated playing, and comparing their moves to previous ones, they discover strategies for using the rules in different ways.
- From analyzing a phenomenon to evaluating its sustainability into the future: Students learn about the critical role of pollination in the ecology of various life systems, including the production of food for humans. They then evaluate how well such a system can sustain itself given the current decline in bee populations; they consider strategies for addressing the problem.

---

## Choices in Depth and Breadth

Besides adjusting for pace and level, teachers also need to consider *depth* and *breadth.* Advanced students who begin a research project, for example, need opportunities to extend their inquiry by reading several books in the library, conducting Internet searches, interviewing people, making diagrams, and recording observations and insights. They thrive in this kind of in-depth study where they can make discoveries and examine related fields for new ideas and sources they would not normally find. Where pace and level focus more on the speed at which a child learns and the degree of difficulty, depth and breadth are more investigative, drawing on a wider range of choices in process (particularly creative or divergent), resources to use, media to consult, and fields of knowledge to explore. Depth and breadth are like archaeological digs, where students keep finding artifacts buried beneath other artifacts and where they apply knowledge and skills from other disciplines to ask questions and pose working theories. Though they take many forms, they distinguish themselves in the following ways:

- They involve and enhance student interests.
- They present questions that can only be answered by inquiring more deeply.
- They provide more and varied sources.
- They integrate disciplines when appropriate and beneficial.
- They allow choices in how students present, produce, or express their findings.

Clearly, the kinds of activities that include depth and breadth could become time consuming and complex, depending on how you structure them. Yet they can also take simpler forms, as shown here.

---

### What can you do for advanced students who need opportunities to study a topic in more depth or to explore a wider range of materials and approaches?

- Would a map-making project enhance their research and writing on immigration in the United States?
- Can you teach them how to analyze local water samples so that they can include this data in an ecology exhibit?
- What other technologies, construction materials, visual aids, or found objects could they use to explore different viewpoints?
- What other subjects or skill areas relate to what they're doing now?

As discussed in the pace and level section, you will likely find a number of students in your class—not formally identified as gifted—who can, nevertheless, achieve more than you thought. Given the chance to choose other ways to discover and interpret new knowledge, they thrive. Depth and breadth learning is often more successful in engaging students' curiosity because it connects to their interests through a wider spectrum of modalities—multimedia, creative, and interdisciplinary.

## Creative Thinking Through the Arts

The arts offer perhaps the richest and most diverse resource for any teacher seeking greater depth and breadth for advanced students. The arts link the world of sensibility and imagination to the world of inquiry, reason, and higher-level thinking. They're also highly flexible—embracing everything from a short simulation to spark a class discussion to a mural project as the culmination of a two-week study project. Most important to the time-constrained teacher, the arts benefit *all* students by giving them alternative ways to process and extend what they're learning.

---

### Arts Applications to Subject Areas

**Music**

Mathematics (calculating, counting, and measuring)

Science (relating sound to image, exploring sound waves, and calculating distance or direction)

Language arts (evoking mood or atmosphere, sensing, imagining, or composing)

Social studies (connecting music traditions to places, times, and cultures)

**Dance**

Mathematics (measuring line and creating patterns)

Science (exploring concepts of force, velocity, and gravity)

Language arts (miming stories or poems and choreographing narrations)

Social studies (movement interpretation of historic event, issue, or situation

**Theater**

Mathematics (interpreting math problems through theater scenes or mime)

Science (imagining and identifying with a species of flora or fauna—a hooded chameleon, a tree, or a carpenter ant)

Language arts (theatrical interpretation of poetry and a readers' theater production)

Social studies (impersonating a famous person or dramatizing a historic debate)

**Visual Arts**

Mathematics (analyzing distance, perspective, ratios, and dimensions)

Science (exploring light and shadow in nature and art or interpreting color, wind, and speed through painting)

Language arts (using paintings or photographs to inspire poetic compositions)

Social studies (relating art composition to map design and using historic art products to analyze social, political, and cultural values and ideas)

Creativity opens the door to discovery. It prompts children to look for ideas where they've never looked before. They see similarities between dissimilar things and differences between similar things; they discover ordinary uses for their most unique inventions and new uses for found objects. They transform a tragedy into a parody and apply mathematical principles to art designs.

Creative strategies take different forms depending on student needs and curriculum goals. Among the many creative processes scholars have explored, perhaps the most widely known (Guilford, 1968; Torrance, 1974; 1979) are as follows:

- Fluency (generating many ideas)
- Flexibility (creating divergent and alternative ideas)
- Originality (producing unique, innovative ideas)
- Elaboration (extending, embellishing, and implementing ideas)
- Transformation (changing or adapting an idea or solution into a different one)
- Evaluation (assessing the viability and usefulness of an idea)

To use the arts most effectively, teachers need to first consider the unique constellation of talent and ability in the learners themselves and then see how an arts process can best stimulate their learning in the unit planned. Drawing on their creative and imaginative energies, students can explore, inquire, and make new discoveries in almost any subject. These are questions worth considering before you proceed:

1. How can the arts support the learning goals I have established in different subjects?

2. What fundamental concepts and skills do students need to learn because of this unit? Where would the arts add depth and breadth and where not?

3. Which of the arts would best serve the learning goal?

4. When should the arts be used—as a catalyst in the beginning, as a process throughout the assignment, or as a final project?

5. How can I apply this process in a way that doesn't take too much teaching time or detract from the primary goal of the lesson?

These are examples of how you can make adjustments in depth and breadth:

---

### Low-Preparation Adjustments

#### *Change Sources and Materials Used*

- *Interdisciplinary.* Information sources within two or more related fields (e.g., science, math, and photography) rather than one; journal entries, video footage, maps, sketchbooks, and blogs instead of just books and articles; instruments and materials from two or three fields (e.g., binoculars, compass, microscope, journal, camera, field guides, or sketch pad)
- *Interests.* Materials and sources related to interests (e.g., personal art supplies, software and Internet sites focused on writing, video camera, costumes and props, theater improvisation books, math games, and recording equipment)
- *Intelligences.* A wide variety of resources reflecting different intelligences of advanced students (spatial, linguistic, logical-mathematical, bodily-kinesthetic, musical, interpersonal, intra-personal, naturalistic, and existential) (Gardner, 1999)
- *Visual arts.* Paints, paintbrushes, and easels; markers; colored pencils; paper in various sizes and colors; magazines; scraps of ribbon or fabric; scissors, glue, paste, and tape; pictures, photo-graphs, posters; camera and film; art books, websites, or bio-graphic sources on visual artists
- *Performing arts.* Simulation games; poems, stories, and novels for readers' theater productions; costumes and props; assistants or coaches with theater experience (other teachers, parents, com-munity volunteers, or personal friends)

*Change Thinking Process*

- From inquiring into historic texts on a particular period to analyzing themes and questions explored by biographies and biographic fiction. From studying and drawing geometric shapes and angles to studying the application of this to identify species of plants and birds.
- From learning about the movements of the major planets in Earth's solar system to comparing this to earlier preheliocentric views of the planets and stars and diagramming/sketching the major misconceptions.
- From writing a report on a rainforest species to interpreting this knowledge through a visual representation its unique ecology.
- From writing a book review to staging a book review show, featuring several students who discuss their views on key questions and including dramatic readings of significant scenes.

## Choices in Grouping

As a teacher, you already know how grouping students together can enhance their growth and learning. At times, direct instruction works best, particularly at the beginning of a unit. Then, student needs and curriculum goals often dictate other arrangements—small learning groups for some activities and independent work for others. Here are a few examples:

*Ability group.* Placing advanced students together in small groups or pairs is highly important not only for their growth but for emotional well-being. Assigning a more difficult version of a class assignment enables them to share strategies and ideas while they work. You can form these groups whenever possible and change the composition as individual needs shift.

*Interest group.* In the course of a project or assignment, you may discover that a number of students are interested in some aspect of the subject you're teaching. In this case, even if you have a mixed-ability group, the high motivation will carry them along and provide activities and resources that benefit everyone. For example, if you have three or four students who love poring over maps, you could incorporate a map-making project that would accommodate the different ability levels in the group.

*Learning style group.* Like all students, advanced learners have preferred ways of processing ideas and information. For example, some students feel more at home with a group of kinesthetic learners who prefer to build, experiment, design, sculpt, move, and dramatize than with those who enjoy reading, writing, and discussion. Sometimes, these groups meet around a learning center in the classroom that focuses on a particular intelligence such as visual/spatial thinking.

## Choices in Independent Work

Most advanced students enjoy working alone, at least part of the time. Independent study is one option. It structures the project to be undertaken with clearly stated accountabilities—not only for the student, but for the teacher and parents as well. Most teachers accomplish this through contracts itemizing specific learning goals, student products, criteria, responsibilities, and deadlines. The independent study option can open a whole world for motivated students who want to explore a favorite topic on their own. More on this option will appear in Chapter 5.

Advanced students can experience independent learning in other, less comprehensive ways for advanced. Two common alternatives are *anchor activities* and *choice boards.* Both of these are quite simple to arrange for students who finish an assignment early and need more challenge. Anchor activities are mini-projects, anchored to the lesson and structured so that students can get their materials and start the process without requiring the teacher's attention. In a unit on African American literature, for example, a child goes to the reading corner with a book on Langston Hughes's childhood that he's going to use to compose a free-verse poem.

A choice board is a chart of activities related to a unit that includes different resources, materials, media, topics, and thinking processes. It takes some initial planning to design choice boards so that students can work independently, using task cards or the simple directions you provide. In a reading unit for young students, for example, a choice might be to create a handmade book or make a story map.

---

### What arrangement would work best for your advanced students in this unit?

- Would they do better working with other high-ability students?
- Are they looking for others who share their passion for theater, biology, or math?
- Do they need some time to work on a project alone?
- What sort of anchor activities could you create for advanced students to do on their own or together?

## K-W-L Charts for Advanced Learners

Because of the focus on prior knowledge and student interest, K-W-L charts are useful for teaching advanced students, and they can adapt to different situations. Once you know what knowledge and ability your students bring to a topic, you can consider small projects that challenge them. The subject chapters (Chapters 6 and 7) provide examples of adjustments you can make at different levels of preparation. For now, consider the process here and how it might work in your classroom.

---

### K-W-L Chart for Advanced Learners

**What student knows about topic**

Facts, concepts, intuitions, and impressions

Level of mastery—grade level or above

Pace of learning—average or above

**What student wants to know**

Student questions, interests, and learning styles

Thinking process—comparing, analyzing, and creating

Arts process—visual and performing

Technology

**What changes to content, process, or product should you make?**

Level and pace, depth and breadth, and grouping and independent work

More challenging sources, higher-level thinking, and creative process

Interdisciplinary options, arts, and other media

Technology

**What student has learned**

New knowledge and concepts; meaningfulness to student

Student evaluation: owning new understanding, increasing motivation

Inspiration to pursue new goals

---

## PARTING THOUGHTS FOR YOUR JOURNEY

*Stay focused on the choices you can provide.* Don't waste time thinking about what you can't do. In any given topic, ask, What else could my advanced students read, research, or analyze? When you're pressed for time, you can at least provide them with a more challenging math puzzler or a more sophisticated book of poems or stories. That may be as much as you can do in some cases. At other times, you can consider thinking process. Creative problem solving turns an easy assignment into a more complex one. Instead of reporting on a historic novel, have them compare the struggles of two main characters and analyze their differing points of view. Instead of calculating the results of a mathematical equation, ask them to find other solutions and rationalize their use. How did they find them, and what benefits do they think their methods have? Allow advanced learners to explore variations of an assignment—either by extending it or by substituting it for something they prefer.

*Engage advanced students in creating alternatives.* This cannot be stressed enough. Motivated, fast-paced learners come to your class with clearly defined interests and learning preferences. They know what they like. The more you allow them to participate in designing their assignments, the more responsible they become. Over time, you develop a shorthand with these students—learning their greatest strengths and anticipating the problems they may have with their assignment. Advanced students who are emotionally mature can do well in independent learning arrangements as long as they know what they're accountable for, can pace themselves well, ask questions when they need assistance, and turn their work in on time.

# Meeting the Needs of Advanced Students

*Strategies to Extend Learning*

"**I**s it possible to attempt larger projects in a manageable way?"

Teachers ask this question somewhat incredulously. Yet it *is* possible to do larger projects in a reasonable way if you've laid the groundwork from Chapter 4 and are practicing some of the changes suggested. The strategies described here depend on your having reached a certain comfort level with those introduced in Chapter 4. Let us say that your classroom provides a variety of multilevel resources and can accommodate both small-group and independent learning activities. This means that you can create more choices for advanced students that build on what they know, adjust the pace and level of instruction to match their abilities, and vary the kind of thinking process they use (e.g., inductive reasoning, analytical, or creative).

In the last chapter, we looked at changes you can make as you teach the lessons you've already planned for the day or week. In this chapter, you extend yourself more, designing alternative learning experiences that may last longer than one class and require more thought and preparation. Those selected here are not how-to formulas, but examples of how you can attempt more ambitious projects in a manageable way.

As you move forward, consider these lists a guide for integrating critical and creative thinking into your units.

| Bloom's Revised Taxonomy (Anderson & Krathwohl, 2001) | Creative Strategies (Guilford, 1968; Torrance, 1974, 1979) |
|---|---|
| • **Remembering** (retrieving, recognizing, and recalling)<br>• **Understanding** (constructing meaning, inferring, and explaining)<br>• **Applying** (using, executing, and implementing)<br>• **Analyzing** (breaking into parts and examining relation to one another)<br>• **Evaluating** (making judgments based on criteria and standards)<br>• **Creating** (putting/ reorganizing elements into a coherent whole) | • **Fluency** (generating many ideas)<br>• **Flexibility** (creating divergent and alternative ideas)<br>• **Originality** (producing unique, innovative ideas)<br>• **Elaboration** (extending, embellishing, and implementing ideas)<br>• **Transformation** (changing or adapting an idea or solution into a different one)<br>• **Evaluation** (assessing the viability and usefulness of an idea) |

You can extend the changes you've already made to create greater academic challenge for your advanced students by following the suggestions in this chapter. Many teachers find that creating more choices for advanced learners has a domino effect, prompting the other students to do more than they had before. Flexible planning helps everyone in the class. The strategies in this chapter, therefore, apply both to the advanced students who sorely need them and to those who are motivated and ready for a new challenge.

## STRATEGIES

We will explore these strategies in this chapter.

1. Compacting

2. Tiered activities

3. Learning centers

4. Creativity/arts integration

5. Grouped instruction

6. Independent study

## 1. Compacting

We already know that advanced students need to learn at a faster pace and higher level. A strategy always worth considering here is *compacting*.

Compacting identifies content and skills in a unit that teachers can eliminate for advanced

> **Compacting—A Three-Step Process**
>
> 1. Assess student mastery
> 2. Skip content mastered
> 3. Design alternatives

learners. The strategy reflects a common concern that gifted children often repeat what they already know. If you have students who consistently finish their assignments early and look inattentive even when you're presenting new material, compacting might be the best answer. You begin by giving them a pretest or assignment that shows what level of knowledge and skill they've mastered in a subject.

---

### To compact the curriculum for a student, you need to

1. Establish what concepts, knowledge, and skills you want all students to master

2. Determine, based on the child's preassessment, what you can delete and what you should adjust for her ability and understanding

3. Explore (with the child) what alternative project he can do

   - A more accelerated and more challenging version of the assignment
   - An extension of an assignment related to the child's interest
   - An independent project in any subject where the child has a special talent or passion

---

After an initial assessment, you can see where students need more challenge and where they require more instruction or practice. One of the advantages of compacting is that it gives students support where they need it without holding them back in areas where they excel. This especially aids talented students with learning disabilities or those from disadvantaged backgrounds, who, for example, may be weak in some skill or content area but who need a chance to develop and express their gifts. In compacting, such a student could practice the math skills she needs with the rest of the class and then move on to more advanced work while the other children learn a concept she has already mastered.

Compacting adapts well to a variety of needs in advanced learners. You might have a student from another country who already knows most of the science planned for the first half of your school year but struggles with the language. Or you could have a child who reads highly sophisticated texts beyond his grade level, but when it comes to writing, he has trouble organizing his ideas. In each case, compacting enables students to skip instruction they do not need, address deficiencies, and continue to develop their strengths through more appropriate learning experiences.

Many teachers create a contract that specifies the project or task a child will do. Here is an example.

---

**Student:** Amanda is an advanced primary student. Highly able in mathematics, she finishes assignments quickly. Though math is not her passion, Amanda became excited when her teacher read *Grandfather Tang's Story* by Ann Tompert (1990) and involved the class in learning the Chinese Tangram pieces.

**Identification of need:** Her teacher observes Amanda as she creates required shapes by flipping, rotating, and assembling Tans. When asked how to make other shapes, she can quickly respond by visualizing the process mentally, even before she moves the pieces. Seeing her enthusiasm for the process and eagerness to try new designs, the teacher works with her to create a more challenging assignment, incorporating her ability in math and her interest in art.

**Assignment:** Write a short story using Tangrams as visual images for the characters. Make sketches of each Tangram character for an artistic representation of her story.

1. Write a story similar to fairy tales or folktales you enjoy.

2. Shape the Tangrams into the characters in your story.

3. Sketch each Tangram shape on paper so you can use it for your art piece.

4. Use paint, magic markers, collages, or any other materials to create a design of your story that includes all your Tangram characters.

---

Once you and your students decide on an alternative project, you can make a timeline for them to complete their work. Some teachers create ready-made project cards or sheets that give advanced children credit for what they've mastered and a list of alternative assignments. If a child loves mathematics and needs more challenge, you can consider other options: starting a small group of more advanced math students for faster-paced instruction, locating math opportunities for gifted students online, arranging for an exceptional student to attend a math class at a higher-grade level.

---

### What about your high-ability students?

Are they repeating what they already know?
(Do they finish assignments early? Are they bored?)

How can you best determine their level of mastery? (Observation, tests, assignments, or class discussion)

What alternative assignment will give them appropriate challenge?

**Consider**

- Learning style
  (hands-on, creative, visual thinking, and mathematical-logical)

- Academic needs
  (inquiry, long-term study, interest-based, and interdisciplinary)

- Creative needs
  (arts integration, flexible thinking, fluency, and invention)

## 2. Tiered Activities

Tiered activities provide a variety of learning paths to accommodate the different levels of ability and experience in your students. They work well when you're teaching fundamental concepts and principles that all students need to understand.

If, for instance, you want your class to explore the environmental impact of American cities on local wildlife, you can design tiered assignments at different levels of skill and ability. You keep the process manageable by not creating more tiered groups than you really need.

Here is an example from a third-grade unit on bird migration:

**Tiered Instruction**

- Teacher designs tiered levels of instruction within one unit.
- Advanced students do a higher-level *version* of an assignment.
- Students can advance to a higher tier if they prove able to do so.

- Group 1 creates a map indicating the migratory route of a particular bird species along the Great Lakes and lists the different threats (e.g., predators, weather, pollution, and cities) they face along the way.
- Group 2 selects one of these threats (e.g., city lights and skyscrapers that confuse nighttime migrating birds), and studies reports on the issue, analyzes current efforts to address the problem, and proposes strategies for ensuring migratory birds a safer passage through the city.

When you use tiered assignments, try to make the different activities equally interesting. Students will quickly see which group is more or less advanced unless the assignments are different enough to make the levels of complexity less obvious. For example, giving the same assignment for two groups but having one read a more difficult book than another will be transparent. But if you're having the students examine point of view in a language arts class, you might divide the groups like this:

- Students in Group 1 choose a position on a current-events issue, imagine belonging to a group affected by the issue, read an article and view footage related to the topic, and write a letter to the editor presenting their point of view. Their composition has to refer to specific facts on the case and present a persuasive defense.
- Students in Group 2 compare the viewpoints of two positions, examine the facts presented in two sources, and analyze the merits and limitations of each. They then summarize each position and write an analysis of the issue that incorporates points from both, but that presents their take on the debate.

---

### What about your class?

Do you see two or more different levels of achievement?

What essential idea, principle, or skill do all students need?

What is the primary goal of this lesson or unit?

What adjustments would make a better fit for advanced students?

**Focus on the following:**

- Essential learning and skill of a subject
- Higher-level thinking used in that discipline
- Opportunities for creative expression/multimedia

---

As seen in Chapter 4, advanced learners not only need the freedom to work at their own pace and level, but they also require *depth* and *breadth*—more opportunities to look deeper into a topic and to draw upon a wider range of resources, materials, and disciplines. Two options described in the following pages are learning centers and arts applications. The first assists advanced students in structuring projects related to their interests. The second uses the power of imaginative and creative thinking to expand learning through integrated arts experiences.

## 3. Learning Centers

Teachers have been designing learning centers for decades, but this section specifically looks at how they can serve as a resource for advanced learners. The first step is to consider how you can make a learning center part of daily life in the classroom. Ideally, a learning center should be a place where students can cycle in and out, as you shift from instructing the whole class to working with small groups to addressing individual problems or questions. Centers create more freedom for you to adapt to individual needs and also increase your students' independence in doing an assignment from beginning to end. Advanced students thrive in center work, as it gives them guidance while also allowing them to follow their creative instincts. At the same time, all students need the skills of self-monitoring, pacing, and planning to undertake more ambitious projects; center activities develop these important life skills.

Try to avoid changing centers frequently. Any situation where planning and designing a process exceed the time students take to *do* it is not practical. Instead, focus all materials on a larger theme or subject (depending on what you feel is the priority), and provide multilevel sources that reflect different learning styles and interests. Design open-ended questions and activities that students can use as catalysts for group or independent work.

Here is an example of how you can structure learning center time.

### Language Arts: Focus on Biography

One option is to have students participate in three rotations. Design your system so that it includes things the students "must do" and those they "can do." A student should always have an activity to be working on. This will help the early finishers who ask, "What do I do now?"

| Small Group With Teacher | Center Work | Independent Seatwork |
|---|---|---|
| Students are grouped based on reading abilities or specific skill needs. The groups are flexible and adjust to individual student needs. Group | Students work alone or with a partner. They remain at the reading/ writing center or visit another area related to their biography study. | Students work at their seats on a variety of independent activities, including the following:<br><br>• Practice sheets<br>• Journal writing |

*(Continued)*

(Continued)

| Small Group With Teacher | Center Work | Independent Seatwork |
|---|---|---|
| activities include the following:<br><br>• Small-group reading instruction with a focus on biographies<br>• Review of key reading questions adjusted for different levels<br>• Higher-level thinking questions for advanced students with writing assignments appropriate for their level | Centers are flexible entities, and can include materials organized in containers (if space is an issue).<br><br>Only a few students should be at a center at one time. Also, only one-third of the class does center work at one time.<br><br>If you notice that advanced students have completed center work, send them back to their seats to get started. Their seatwork should reflect their ability and be adjusted accordingly. | • Word study<br>• Poetry journal<br>• Assigned reading<br>• Seasonal or research projects<br><br>Advanced students can choose other activities that reflect their abilities and experience.<br><br>• Reading/researching<br>• Organizing primary and secondary sources<br>• Exploring questions from biography study<br>• Poetry<br>• Biography map<br>• Essay<br>• Creative product—rap, podcast, or collage |

Center work is only beneficial if all students can achieve some measure of independence and monitor their progress. For many teachers, the two lingering challenges are (1) dealing with an increased noise level and (2) fielding the barrage of questions that often arise when students try something new. To deal with these problems, try to establish firm rules on talking that are clear to everyone. For example, you may decide that small groups can talk at a low volume, those at the center(s) can share at a whisper level, and those working independently should remain quiet (unless receiving assistance from a peer or the teacher). To avoid the chaos of constant interruption, you could create a routine for responding to questions (e.g., students put their name on a running list at the front of the room)—so that you're able to assist in an orderly way.

## 4. Creativity/Arts Integration

Drawing on creative thinking and the arts to introduce a topic can turn a somewhat routine class into a highly imaginative one, where all students feel they have something to think about, learn, and give. As long as you align arts activities with fundamental learning goals, you can open a new unit for students to respond in more creative ways. Here is an example.

### If Trees Could Speak

*To Begin*

Use a K-W-L chart to explore what general knowledge students have about trees.

- Observe and describe the difference between early and late wood. Use hand lenses.
- Guess about the age of the tree, and then determine the actual age by counting the rings.
- Examine the different rings in the trunk and what they say about a tree's past and history.
- Identify rings that represent the years the child, the child's parents, and the child's grandparents were born or years of historic importance. (Remember that the youngest rings are on the outside.)
- Have older students identify the narrowest rings, then check precipitation records to see if these coincide with years of low rainfall.

**Using the Arts**

- Teacher aligns art process to learning goals in a unit
- Teacher uses an arts activity to tap the potential of advanced kinesthetic and/or visual learners
- Teacher integrates the arts for different purposes within a unit
  - Catalyst activity at the beginning—visual art images and sound recordings as prompts for composing free verse
  - Integrated throughout the unit to explore, analyze, interpret—readers' theater process to examine a historic event

*Imaginative Response*

Every year, trees grow new wood in the layer just beneath their bark. Students can see a year's growth because wood produced during the first part of the growing season (early wood) tends to be lighter in color than the denser wood produced at the close of the season (late wood). The width of a given ring reflects the tree's growth rate in a particular year. Since growth rate depends largely on precipitation (or the lack of it) during the growing season, the widths of tree rings can be used to reconstruct rainfall patterns in the past and, in particular, to identify periods of drought. Most trees (like people) grow fastest when they are young, and this must also be taken into consideration when interpreting ring widths.

After exploring different tree species, climates, and environments, the students choose a year or period that they can describe based on the rings. You can then pose questions such as the following:

- What kind of land surrounds you?
- Are there other trees near you?
- What sort of weather and environment surrounds you?
- What do you remember about this period?
- Describe your surroundings—where did you stand, and what did you see?
- What was happening in your area at that time in history?

The children respond by writing and also by sketching, painting, or composing art pieces. Because they are combining scientific knowledge with their imagination, students can choose different genres to suit their purpose—short stories, essays, autobiographies, or poems. The possibilities are endless. Once you touch the creative potential of students, they respond almost immediately with original ideas. In our experience, integrating the arts in this way not only enables them to make discoveries about a phenomenon such as trees but also to experience its beauty and artistry. An interesting process begins to happen. The students explore different ways of expressing scientific facts creatively, and then their creative ideas impel them to dig deeper into the science behind their stories, poems, drawings, sketches, and dramatizations. Try to imagine a student who creates a collage comparing the tree's roots to people's roots, or a child who writes a poem about witnessing a historic moment in time *as the tree*, or another child who sketches a series of diagrams about four different years in the life of the tree with journal entries describing them. A creative process like this—whether it involves the imagination or an aha moment of discovery—always opens the door to our students' minds in ways we cannot predict.

We close this chapter with small groups and independent learning. Helping advanced students almost always involves one or the other, as they respond to two fundamental needs:

1. To learn with similarly gifted peers with whom they can share ideas and interests (group)

2. To immerse themselves in projects where they can explore, design, innovate, and draw on the full power of their imagination and intellect (independent)

## 5. Grouped Instruction

Do gifted students need to work in a group? We touched on this in Chapter 4. The stereotype of the lone and brilliant achiever is myth.

Advanced learners often yearn for a community of people who understand and accept them as they are. Without any contact with other advanced students, they tend to downplay their interests and abilities, knowing that they will become isolated and alone if they stick out from the crowd. Grouped with others like them, however, these children can explore, discover, and analyze ideas with those who feel the same curiosity and excitement. Research has consistently shown that greater academic growth results when advanced learners can share strengths, talents, and interests with like-minded peers (Kulik & Kulik, 1990; Winebrenner & Devlin, 2001).

To pursue this option, consider these guidelines:

---

### Guidelines for Grouped Instruction

- Design assignments that the groups will be able to tackle with minimum input from you. They should provide enough challenge to stretch the students' abilities in new ways, but not so much that they can't work on their own.
- Give each group instructions and examples to guide the process, but with a wide latitude to discover their own methods.
- For advanced students, assure them that, while they are together to share their discoveries and ideas, they are free to pursue their inspiration, wherever it leads.
- Be clear about what each individual student is responsible for—what she must do and produce by the end of a process.

---

Students can join different kinds of groups depending on the learning need, the subject, and the assigned task—for example, one for those gifted in math (e.g., group forms during math instruction to work on alternative assignments) and another for those who share a love of art and design (e.g., group forms to design a map display for a social studies project). The key is to maintain flexibility so that you can adjust group composition in response to the growth and needs of individual students. In this way, you can create a classroom where students with different learning styles, interests, and abilities can benefit from shared experiences with like-minded peers.

---

### How do you group your students?

How often do your advanced students work together?

What arrangements do you use? Pairs? Small groups?

What sorts of groups do your advanced students join?

What benefits to their growth do you see?

---

## 6. Independent Study

Some students need more time to work alone, and there are individual cases that require a significantly different approach in some subjects. In the last chapter, we explored some of the simpler ways to meet this need such as in anchor activities and choice boards. For students who need more, you can design an independent study. Most teachers accomplish this through some kind of contract or written agreement that helps them to manage the process.

Contracts for independent study are handy aids in a variety of other strategies such as compacting, tiered instruction, research projects, and creative work. Your main objective is to establish clear goals, priorities, and instructions and to structure the project in such a way that students know exactly what to do at each stage. The following guidelines are just suggestions, which you can adapt to your classroom.

---

### Independent Study Guidelines

- Identify what students should know (facts), understand (concepts), and be able to do (skills) by the end of the project.
- Identify a result in the form of a product (e.g., a poem, an experiment, a report, a map, or a combination of products).
- List expectations for content (what is to be learned), process (how it's to be done), and product (tangible result that demonstrates learning).
- Determine support you may need to provide along the way (goal setting, brainstorming, timelines, etc.).
- Adjust assignments based on student ability, mastery of subject, interest, and learning style.
- Mentor the student when needed.

---

This process can be as in-depth as is best for your students and you. Bear in mind that although students need specific goals and directions, you don't have to structure every step if the students have enough guidance to support their process. Here is an example:

**Project:** To create a parody of Cinderella that uses some of the techniques the student has learned about satire and parody.

*This is what she wants to learn:*

- The elements of a good parody—how parody can poke fun while simultaneously revealing important ideas or truths

- The different ways she can turn the Cinderella story into a parody of teenage mall culture
- Best techniques for writing a parody

### This is what she needs to do:

1. Read two parodies that she likes.

2. Clarify techniques of parody: *diminution, inflation,* and/or *juxtaposition.*

3. Decide on the object of her parody—social behavior or institution.

4. Decide on the goal of her parody: How does she want to affect the readers?

5. Brainstorm some plot ideas.

6. Plot her parody to see how it works.

### Criteria

- The story draws on her analysis of cartoons, caricatures, films, television shows, and at least two books, focusing on the question, What strategy is at work here?
- The parody illustrates *diminution, inflation,* and/or *juxtaposition* to create its effect.
- The story has a strong message or point of view about a condition, behavior, or institution.
- The story has a strong beginning, middle, and end; is vividly told; and maintains suspense throughout.
- The story includes a plan for revision based on feedback from a writing partner and conference with the teacher.

A process like this satisfies the need of advanced learners to immerse themselves in something beyond the time-constrained tasks of everyday assignments. Through her independent study, the student analyzes the techniques of satire and how they operate in different contexts. She applies techniques found in other media (books, television, film, or cartoon) and composes an original parody.

### Mentorship

Mentorships are ideal for some advanced students. Not all can handle the responsibility or sustain the motivation and focus required, however. Some people assume that with talent and ability, any promising student would benefit from a mentoring situation, but this is not true. For those self-starters, though, a mentorship can offer a much more advanced and rapid pace of instruction. This option has proven especially helpful for highly gifted students. A fourth grader who writes like a high school or college student can advance her ability far more by working one-on-one with an author who can give her the feedback and support she needs. A fifth grader with a passion for South American reptiles will blossom under the tutelage of a researcher with firsthand experience in the rain forests of Costa Rica. Mentors can reveal a new universe for an exceptional child, providing the direction and guidance that only specialists can. Nobel Laureate Joshua Lederberg spoke of the frustration he felt as a young person in school: "My teachers were wonderfully supportive but they didn't know what to do with me. Nobody took me in charge, gave me a sense of what to do. I could have used more guidance on what to read, how to structure what was going on . . ." (Subotnik, 1995, p. 218).

Finding mentors is not always easy, particularly as you are looking for those who can provide appropriate content, activities, and resources for advanced learners. If no one in the school district can assume the role, some teachers find that they can search universities, businesses, art schools, and studios to discover people who can give mentees the right kind of experience. In this respect, *telementoring*—otherwise known as virtual mentoring or e-mentoring—has become a useful and more convenient alternative (Nash, 2001). Teachers can consult The National Mentoring Partnership (http://www.mentoring.org) for guidance on finding mentors and developing advanced course content for particularly gifted students. Though nothing can quite replace the presence of a real human being, telementoring has distinct advantages (Siegle & McCoach, 2005, pp. 483–484). With access to the Internet, geographic distance and scheduling problems can no longer hinder a promising student who could otherwise never hope to find a mentor ready to open the world to them.

## PARTING THOUGHTS FOR YOUR JOURNEY

*Try large goals in small steps.* Remember that you are building from the steps you took in the last chapter. It is a challenge to launch a child on an independent study project without first trying smaller, independent events—a writing activity at a learning center or a short fact-finding mission on a volcano to add to a science class discussion. Some independent studies can last for a week or more. Start with one- or two-day projects. The same applies to tiered activities. If it takes too much time to design three tiers within a unit to meet everyone's needs, then do two. For the truly advanced students, you can add another dimension if needed. There is no right path other than feeling your way, observing what happens, and adapting as you go.

*Remember to start larger projects in a topic you know well.* We've said this before but it bears saying again. One reason some teachers get frustrated is because they try a more challenging process in a new unit. If you're unsure about how an independent study or a tiered assignment or an arts project will work, try it first in a unit you know extremely well. Otherwise, the planning process will seem excessive, and you'll be juggling too many elements at once.

*You don't have to be an artist to use the arts.* Teachers don't always believe us, but anyone can use the arts in the classroom! Try some of the ideas presented here on a small scale. Consult with an art teacher, a musician, or a theater friend if you feel uncertain about your plan or need moral support. The level of student motivation and interest by itself is worth the effort. When aligned with curriculum standards and designed to inspire flexible thinking, discovery, and innovation in all students, , the arts become an abundant and versatile resource for classroom teachers. We have seen nothing in the classroom that ignites student learning in quite the same way.

# Teaching Advanced Students in Language Arts and Social Studies

**A**nnie Proulx once said, "The reader writes the story," hinting at the process of reading as inherently active and creative. For gifted educator and author Jerry Flack (2000), "Reading is the space capsule that allows gifted children to reach for the stars, pursuing their education well beyond the confines of lockstep progression through the traditional curriculum" (p. 22).

We have combined language arts and social studies in this chapter because the two develop similar skills and thinking processes. It can be useful to consider these fundamental areas as we explore different strategies for teaching advanced learners. Both subjects demand a considerable amount of reading, for example. When they read, students

- connect what they know to new information;
- question themselves and the texts;
- discuss and debate ideas, impressions, interpretations;
- visualize, imagine, and make inferences;
- distinguish most important ideas;
- synthesize information and ideas from different sources; and
- respond to text through essays, stories, biographies, and poems.

Internalizing the structure and style of various texts in language arts, advanced students discover new thoughts and questions as they write.

Metaphoric language, voice, tone, and style become their writer's brush. They thread together ideas from a book, a website, a magazine, and an interview; make connections between them; analyze possible meanings; and interpret the results. Creativity permeates this process, as it involves gathering sources, constructing meanings, engaging the senses, learning stories, studying words and sounds, and composing texts of their own. They become *thinking* readers and writers who need a wider range of sources and choices than most standard curricula provide.

Shifting to the social studies, these same students also need opportunities to follow their curiosity—to build on their advanced knowledge and skill as readers, researchers, debaters, analysts, and writers. The social studies provide this. Students

- analyze cause-and-effect relationships (history, environment, politics, and economics);
- conduct research and inquiry (deciphering primary and secondary sources, analyzing and evaluating evidence);
- examine interpretations and points of view;
- synthesize information and create hypotheses;
- debate positions and write reports; and
- compose persuasive essays, poems, posters, and podcasts.

For many advanced learners, the social studies offer vast and enticing explorations to other times and places. Even during their earliest years, they're on a search for distant shores and epochs. We find them, as the first author found a three-year-old, in a rock shop calmly explaining to his father what "prehistoric" means and what kind of habitat pterodactyls need. With a curiosity about the world around them, advanced students quickly become adept at conducting inquiries and creating vivid representations of what they know. We met a child who designed what he called a "botanical trail map" of his favorite forest preserve; it provided information on the plants and trees that hikers could find on the different trails. Another child one author knows, who spent a year with her father in the Middle East, became fascinated by the relationship of architecture to culture and history, and announced one day, at the age of 11, that she wanted to become a specialist in "indigenous architecture."

So the question becomes, How do you respond to the needs of your advanced students in language arts and social studies while pursuing the curriculum and learning standards given you? How do you set priorities in such a way that you can provide the challenge they need without undue stress and strain on your time and resources?

The next chart should help clarify the most important needs of your advanced students *at this point*. Start with what you know of a student so far. Based on your observation and assessment, what does this child most need? Where do you see this most? What areas of your teaching day and in what subjects can you be more flexible and creative in adjusting a learning process? How might you approach this?

---

### What-Where-How Priority List

1. **What** are the greatest needs of my advanced learners right now?

**Identify needs, interests, learning styles**

> Observation
> Assignments
> K-W-L charts
> Tests
> Talent days
> Feedback (parents and other school personnel)

2. **Where** can I address them at this point?

**Focus on big ideas, concepts, and skills**

> Language arts
> Literature (poetry, nonfiction, biography, stories, novels, and essays)
> Writing (essays, reports, poems, and stories)
> Social studies
> Skills (map-making, researching, and outlining)
> Thinking (interpreting, comparing, analyzing, and composing reports)

3. **How** do I address their needs in an effective yet reasonable way?

**Create choices with challenge**

> Faster pace
> Higher-level thinking (taxonomies)
> Creative thinking
> The arts
> Grouping/pairs
> Independent learning

---

This list aims to streamline the process of planning so that you can adjust as you go. For example, if you have a student who wants to do more with a research topic than a short essay, you can provide direction for her to extend her inquiry and give her time to work during class periods she can afford to miss. Relating this to the previous chart, you identify *what* this student most needs in your social studies class (more in-depth study), you decide *where* she can conduct her research and writing (during periods of review), and you explore with the student *what* alternative assignment she wants to undertake (e.g., lengthier report that draws on more sources or multimedia production).

From the American Heritage Dictionary, the word "curriculum" comes from the Latin verb meaning "to run" (*currere*), pointing to a journey that is traveled rather than a series of facts that are acquired. Seeing your units this way is freeing, as it casts students more as travelers—each moving toward the same destination but needing different routes to get there. Writing a position paper on a current event, for example, may become a reporting process for one group of students and an in-depth analysis for another.

The question always is, *What resources and strategies can best enable you to respond to those whose greatest challenge is the lack of challenge?*

To return to the What-Where-How Priority List, you begin with the learning needs of your advanced students. From their work in the classroom, you've become familiar with their abilities, interests, and special skills. You know what they love to do, how they best learn, and where they can get in their own way (e.g., by being perfectionists, by not pacing themselves well, etc.). If they're ahead in *all* subjects, then you begin wherever you can most easily make changes. For example, if you know you have several exceptional writers, you start there.

As they plan, most teachers try to organize their units around big ideas and fundamental skills that reflect the standards and learning benchmarks in each subject area.

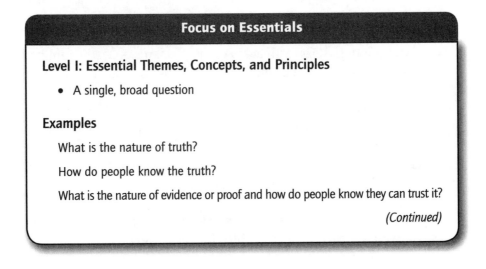

### Focus on Essentials

**Level I: Essential Themes, Concepts, and Principles**

- A single, broad question

**Examples**

What is the nature of truth?

How do people know the truth?

What is the nature of evidence or proof and how do people know they can trust it?

*(Continued)*

(Continued)

**Level II: Information, Concepts, and Skills Tied to Learning Standards**

- A few student-centered questions

**Examples**

If someone says, "I heard it on T.V.," do you believe it is true?

How can you find out if a report is true? What do you have to know?

How do you know which sources are reliable and which are not?

The focus on essentials is what gives you wriggle room for making adjustments where you need them.

For example, a unit on the multiple levels of meaning in written and oral language is a central idea—big enough to provide both for your most advanced and most challenged students. In social studies, doing research on an event or phenomenon—distinguishing primary from secondary sources, determining their reliability, and analyzing and interpreting what they mean—is an essential process and embraces students over a wide spectrum of ability and skill.

As you plan, ask yourself two levels of questions—essential and unit (Heacox, 2002). Besides the ones in the chart, here is another example from a second-grade classroom: "What are folktales, and how are they different from all other tales or stories?" Unit questions evolve from this broad question and target specific information, concepts, and skills. Examples could include the following: What folktales do you know? Why do you think they're called folktales? Who do you think made up folktales? Often, these questions tie in with curriculum standards. Keep the number of questions relatively low. For many teachers, unit questions help them structure the class.

Next are some examples used by teachers we know that illustrate how to create more appropriate learning experiences for advanced students in the regular classroom. They're included only to inspire your ideas. As you consider them, think about the elements first described in Chapter 3 and how you might incorporate them into your units:

- Choices for high-ability students provided in assignments or projects
- Accelerated learning incorporated for fast learners

- Creative process and use of the arts integrated wherever possible
- Student interests emphasized
- Peer collaboration in group projects encouraged where appropriate
- Technology incorporated
- Independent learning allowed
- Self-assessment skills taught to monitor progress

## EXAMPLES

### Literature Circles

Adapted from Gish, Pam. In Smutny, J. F., & von Fremd, S. E. *Igniting Creativity in Gifted Learners, K-6: Strategies for Every Teacher.* Copyright © 2009, Corwin. pp. 54–55.

---

**What-Where-How Priority List**

1. **What** are the greatest needs of my advanced learners right now?

   Peer collaboration
   Analytical thinking
   Creativity
   Interpretive response

2. **Where** can I address them at this point?

   Reading and discussion of literature

3. **How** do I address their needs in an effective yet reasonable way?

   Have students work in pairs or small groups
   Allow them to choose more challenging book
   Guide discussion through higher-level thinking questions
   Stimulate creative and interpretive responses through arts, writing, and other media

---

### Benefits

Literature circles allow advanced students the independence they need to develop their analytical and interpretive abilities as readers. When given challenging themes and discussion questions, they can reflect more deeply as they read, interpret, and respond to books. Collaboration is at the heart of this process. Students gain more insight as they construct meaning with other readers. Finally, literature circles guide advanced students to a much more comprehensive understanding of a text through structured discussion as well as written and artistic response.

## Level

Primary, intermediate, and middle school levels

## Description

In literature circles, small groups of students discuss a piece of literature in depth. Student discussion covers a range of topics from characterization and plot to point of view, theme, writing craft or style, personal experience (related to the text), and different interpretations of meaning. The benefit of literature circles for teachers is the flexibility. Different roles are suggested for discussion, but individual teachers select those that best serve their students and may even change or add a role as needed.

Many classrooms begin with some variation of the following roles:

*Discussion director.* This student heads the discussion. He focuses on big ideas in the text, addresses questions related to these ideas, and tries to connect to the overarching themes and concepts woven through the story, novel, or essay.

*Illuminator.* This student chooses specific passages she considers key to the text. They should stand out for being entertaining, dramatic, or meaningful in some way. The student points a light beam on the major dilemma or issue that jumps out at her.

*Illustrator.* This student selects a scene, a concept, a theme, or a characterization as the raw material for an art piece (drawing, cartoon, painting, etc.). The visual piece becomes a catalyst for exploring the interpretation's meaning and significance as a response to the text.

*Connector.* This student links what he is reading to an experience or situation outside the classroom. This could include other texts or sources the student remembers.

*Word wizard.* While reading the text, this student explores the words she finds significant or notable in some way and shares them with the other students.

*Summarizer.* This student explores the main points, themes, or plot twists of a text and the fundamental questions that occurred to him while reading. He presents a summary of each reading assignment to assist the discussion.

The teacher uses roles to start and then dispenses with them when students become more engaged in the process. For advanced students particularly, these roles can be restrictive if continued for an extended period. Even at the beginning, they may prefer combining roles rather than confining themselves to one narrow focus.

Advanced students also need a wider range of processes and sources to use than those outlined in discussion group roles. So an illustrator may do a short video, a connector may create a design or text collage, and a word wizard may write a free-verse poem. In addition, these students need higher level and creative thinking processes to guide their questions and discussion. Primary teacher Pam Gish, who describes her process here, incorporates Bloom's taxonomy (Anderson & Krathwohl, 2001) to raise the bar for all students, particularly her advanced readers (Smutny & von Fremd, 2009, pp. 54–55):

In the literature circle paradigm, groups are formed either formally by the teacher or informally by the students around a topic or book. Each participant has a specific role in the group session, which rotates. The roles I use are connector, questioner, word wizard, illustrator, and character analyzer, and they all write chapter summaries. Students are responsible for reading the given assignment, preparing for that role, and sharing it when the group meets. At the end of the meeting, they make a new reading assignment and meeting time. Groups should be independent, with the teacher acting as facilitator and mentor. This takes some training and modeling by the teacher and experienced groups.

### Preparation

I spend one or two sessions on each role, presenting it, reading a short story, and modeling how it works, and then I have the students practice it themselves and share. After the training is finished, I prefer to group my students by reading level to ensure that their book choices are manageable but still challenging. I offer the group a variety of books at that level and let them come to a consensus. They then receive a packet that contains a description of each role with examples and specific role pages to complete.

### Higher-Level Thinking

One of the most critical roles to promote higher-level thinking and discussion is that of the questioner. This is where the terms from Bloom's taxonomy (Anderson & Krathwohl, 2001) play a crucial role. I explain the different levels and give them examples from each one. They help me decide whether a question is skinny (one-word answer) or fat (thought-provoking answer). This list is printed in their packet, and as I rotate between the groups that are meeting, I take time to ask them who has had the fattest questions. When they are doing their reading and working, I rotate around

> *the room offering suggestions and encouragement. With my highest groups, I highlight the application, analysis, synthesis, and evaluation words and require them to use at least one when developing their questions. They soon grow to love the lively discussions, and the quality of divergent thinking and creative ideas has astounded me. This spreads to the other groups as well, and it goes far beyond the standard teacher questions. Of course, they often are carried away and need teacher assistance to get back on task—but the excitement about these reading groups makes it difficult to go back to the standard format.*

### Extension

A natural development from literature circles for advanced students is reader's theater. Many of the analytical and interpretive questions explored in the literature circles can become catalysts for a theatrical interpretation. Reader's theater challenges advanced learners in these ways:

- The students select the most critical passages of a text, a process that can become a wonderful exercise in higher-order thinking.
- They choose one student to be the narrator and then the others select the characters they would like to dramatize, read, or mime. If more than one student wishes to assume a role, the group considers creative options for sharing roles.
- Students explore how to dramatize important scenes in a story. For example, the actors decide which scenes should be staged with dialogue from the story and which scenes should be narrated and mimed.
- Students take ownership of the story by interpreting character motivation, studying plot structure, and examining point of view.

Reader's theater enables advanced students to read literature they love, share insights, interpret meanings, write, and collaborate with peers in re-creating scenes from their imaginations. Without the burden of having to memorize lines or create props and sets, students can focus more on the creative process of translating one medium—a text—into another one—live theater.

### Word Exploration

---

Adapted from Flack, Jerry. In Smutny, J. F., & von Fremd, S. E. *Igniting Creativity in Gifted Learners, K-6: Strategies for Every Teacher.* Copyright © 2009, Corwin. pp. 46–47.

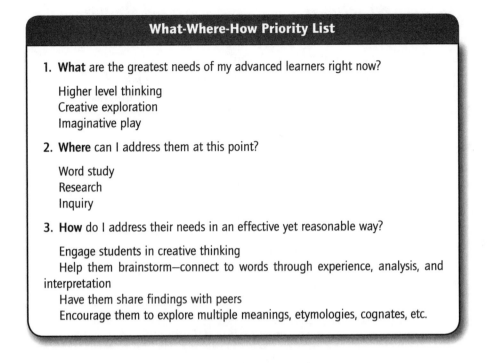

## Rationale

Teacher Jerry Flack has found that the study of words expands the world of language for advanced learners. As they discover etymology with all its depths and nuances of meaning, they relish the odd word, the unusual word, and, of course, the big word. They trace the origins of *Spessartite, stichomythia, stridulation, sublimity, sumptuousness, surreptitiousness,* and *symmetry!* Learning about words, Flack notes, is always a stimulating and creative challenge.

## Description

Flack recommends these steps (Smutny & von Fremd, 2009, pp. 46–47):

*Brainstorm.* Creative explorations with words may begin when students brainstorm words they enjoy and that possess rich connotative value. Ask students to cite their favorite words, or suggest words (e.g., pride, giftedness, or spiritual) and seek related student definitions, impressions, and experiences. Sample words that contain rich multiple layers of meaning include *beauty, genius, patriotism, femininity, masculinity, power, nature, talent, creativity, youth, wisdom, honor, enthusiasm,* and *freedom.*

*Explore.* Encourage students to select a single word, preferably an abstract noun, and begin thorough investigations and interaction with their words of choice. Tell creative students to avoid dictionary definitions at the beginning. Invite a more creative and personal approach to each individual's nuanced understanding of a word.

*Create.* Invite talented students to create a *biography* of a word. The following steps, addressed directly to students, provide fine guidance, but creative teachers should definitely feel free to expand on these choices.

## Steps

1. Write your definition of a single, important word. What do you think the word means?

   Collect several photographs, postcards, news stories, and many diverse materials associated with your chosen word. Use the media you have found to create a visual collage. Give your chosen word a creative artistic appearance.

   Write about a personal experience in which your word plays a role. For example, recall a time when you demonstrated *bravery.*

   Write a poem, story, or song that illustrates the connotation or import of your special word. If your favorite word is a season of the year, you might write a haiku as a tribute to it.

   Engage in demographic research. Ask a minimum of five other people what they believe your chosen word means. Try to ask people from different generations as well as class peers. Record all responses in your word biography journal.

   Be inventive. Create an entirely new word that might be included in a dictionary as a synonym for your word choice.

   Use a dictionary. After you have explored the personal, emotional, or connotative meaning of a word, consult a dictionary to note how scholars have defined your word. The dictionary definition of a word is referred to as its denotative meaning. If many definitions are noted in the dictionary, record two to four of your favorite options in your word journal.

   Begin a creative word journal. Compile all of the previous words and images in a special journal, notebook, or portfolio. Be sure to use media of choice to fashion a highly artistic cover for your creative biography of a word. When your word investigation is complete, you will have an inclusive history and meaning of a special word.

## Extensions

Jerry Flack's suggestions for word exploration can open the door to other forms of expression.

*Historic travelogue.* Students do a historic travelogue that tells how and where a word was born and the changes it underwent as it migrated through time and across continents. An example might be the word "bailiwick," which began as an old legal term from England, combining *bailie* and *wick*. *Bailie* means *bailiff*, an administrative official, and comes from Middle English and Old French *bailli*. The *wick* part comes from the Old English *wic*, meaning dwelling, farm, or town. In the mid-15th century, the word *bailiwick* referred to the district under a bailiff's jurisdiction. In the mid-19th century, the term migrated to America, where it came to mean a person's sphere of responsibility or expertise. Using the word as a catalyst, students can create a visual design or a cartoon, or compose a short written piece on the theme, "What's your bailiwick?"

Advanced students enjoy learning how historic, political, and cultural influences affect words and their meanings. Language is alive and continually evolves. Once a decade, the Merriam-Webster dictionary adds new words and revises definitions of old ones. A word study should always include the history behind its uses and transformations. Other examples might be the following:

- **Nice.** A word that used to be an insult! In the 13th century, it meant foolish or stupid and through the centuries, it could mean extravagant, strange, shy, or coy. Today, a "nice" person is none of these.
- **Silly.** Back in the 11th century, "silly" signified blessed or happy. It gradually changed to refer to someone who is pious and innocent, later degrading to a feeble-minded person. The latter then led to the foolish characteristic we think of today.

*Slang study.* Many slang words are obviously too offensive for students to explore. But some have found their way to the dictionary and are fun for those who enjoy their expressive character and connection to specific subcultures and times. Here are a couple of examples:

- **Headbanger.** A hard rock musician and fan. The word was first coined during a 1969 Led Zeppelin tour in the United States when fans in the front row banged their heads on the stage in time with the music. This is not certain, however.
- **Prairie Gophering.** A wonderful term that refers to people in office buildings who peer above their cubicles while working.

Most students have seen slang words circulate and then fade among their friends in short periods. Including slang enables them to explore the living quality of language and track its roots. They can ask their friends and themselves questions such as these:

- How and when did we start using this word?
- How do we think it might have started?
- What do we like about it? (What does it "say" that another word doesn't?)
- Where do we see it used most (other friends, movies, raps, or songs)? Is this word as popular as before and if not, what other words are people starting to use?

Students then create definitions, based on the format of dictionaries. They explain why the publishers of a new dictionary should include their word. Why is it important, and how do they know it will last?

### Performing the Word

Word study also lends itself to live performance—a medium particularly beneficial to kinesthetic learners. A group of advanced students can use the words they have researched to create performance pieces: live poetic "plays" on a word with mime; dramatizations of multiple meanings; humorous combinations of chosen words performed in brief, improvised sketches (see Resources for information on using improvisation in the classroom).

### Free-Verse Poetry

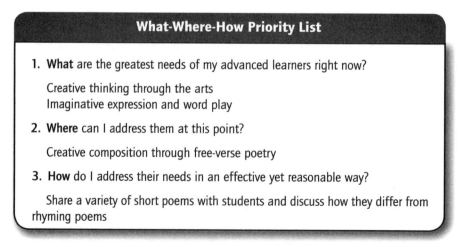

**What-Where-How Priority List**

1. **What** are the greatest needs of my advanced learners right now?

   Creative thinking through the arts
   Imaginative expression and word play

2. **Where** can I address them at this point?

   Creative composition through free-verse poetry

3. **How** do I address their needs in an effective yet reasonable way?

   Share a variety of short poems with students and discuss how they differ from rhyming poems

> Give students visual materials (e.g., posters, photographs, or paintings) as catalysts for their writing
>
> Invite students to compose a group poem in response to visual art with each child adding a line
>
> Have them choose a line, image, or idea from the group poem to create another free-verse composition

## Rationale

Free-verse poetry is highly versatile. Through poetic composition, advanced students can explore expressive language within a range of subjects and topics. Like painters, poets combine feeling, texture, thought, and imagery to understand and interpret the world around them. Not only can advanced students practice poetic writing as a medium for learning and self-expression but also use their compositions as catalysts for other inventions—paintings, songs, stories, and dramatizations. Creative poets tend to express themselves in more than one modality.

## Description

*Expose students to free-verse poems.* Teaching free verse only works well if students have access to the diversity of poetic writing in free verse. This exposure can encompass different subjects—for example, the nature poems of someone like Mary Oliver as well as the evocative verse of a writer like Sonia Sanchez, who draws deeply on the speech and language of her community. For advanced students, poetry selections should include adult verse as well because they can handle a more sophisticated level of writing.

*Offer catalysts.* Students need some kind of catalyst to inspire a poetic response. Nothing is more difficult than facing a blank page; whereas, a painting, print, poster, video/audio recording, book, or website immediately ignites the imagination. Students can improvise with source materials, exploring and playing with them. They interpret the gestures, perspectives, and images in paintings; they respond to the sound of rain, the urgent honking of rush hour traffic, or the voices of people shuffling through a train station; they ponder character motivation in a story and analyze its historic and cultural worlds; and they relate these sources to their experiences, thoughts, and feelings.

*Create a class poem.* Working as a group to create a poem helps timid students start the process. In the context of literature (whether fiction or nonfiction), for example, the teacher can ask for students' impressions, feelings, and interpretations. A poster, picture, or video recording can also inspire ideas for writing. The teacher encourages students to think about the atmosphere of a picture or recording—the images, sounds, and sensations—and asks them to imaginatively step into the world of that picture or recording. She can begin by asking questions such as these:

- If you walked into this painted world, where would you be standing?
- What would you see, feel, or hear?
- What colors leap out at you? Make you want to run and hide? Make you want to play a game?
- If you look carefully at the people (or animals) in this picture, what are they doing?
- If you could free them from the painting, where would they go?
- If you were to think of the picture as music or sound, what would you hear?
- If you sat in the middle of it, what textures and temperatures would you feel (cold, smooth, warm, sticky, damp, rough, etc.)?
- What does this painting say to you and what do you want to say to it (or to someone in it)?

The same process can be done with music or sound recordings. As students' minds percolate with ideas and hands start popping up, the teacher asks for phrases or lines to put on the board. When a child offers a phrase, the teacher responds, "OK! This is the beginning of our free-verse poem. Now can I have another? What else do you see? What do you imagine you might hear or feel if you could be there?" Emboldened by the first child's offering, more children respond. Soon, everyone wants to add a line.

*Guidance.* While students write, the teacher guides students to different sources as the need arises. He circulates around the room, helping writers focus on the details that bring their poems to life:

- Notice the picture of X (person or animal); what is she staring at? What exists outside the lines of the painting? What does the expression on the face or body tell you? What do you imagine has just happened before this picture was taken/painted?
- Pick a color, shape, or something that you like the most about this painting, print, photograph, or film. Write whatever words or phrases come to you.
- Listen to this music or sound recording while you study a painting. What does the music or sound tell you about this scene? Close your eyes and imagine movements around you, the touch of them against your skin and face, the smells.

- Look at this environment. Imagine living there yourself. What sounds do you think you'd hear? Walk around in the painting/print and imagine what you would see, who you would talk to, and what you might smell as you passed the little shops.

*Creative extensions.* When students engage in creative composition in this way, they become inspired to write in vivid and evocative language. They can also extend their free-verse poems to other modes of expression. Multimedia projects, based on the poems, could include stories, drawings, diagrams, maps, cartoons, podcasts, videos, songs, and dramatizations. The children choose whatever media they feel would best enhance their poems. The teacher could ask, "What would be the best way to build on the atmosphere of your poem? What will help you extend the mood or meaning of your poem? How can you make the heavy air more intense for the reader? How can you give us the feel of cool, fresh rain? Can you do it with collage? A cartoon? A story? Another poem? A song?" Once students gain some practice writing poems, they can use the medium more freely, applying it to any situation that lends itself to poetic interpretation. Because of the demand to distill their thoughts in precise and powerful language, advanced writers often find it cathartic to give creative voice to strong feelings or opinions.

## Podcasting

Adapted from Funke, Courtland. In Smutny, J. E., & von Fremd, S. E. *Igniting Creativity in Gifted Learners, K-6: Strategies for Every Teacher.* Copyright © 2009, Corwin. pp. 59–61.

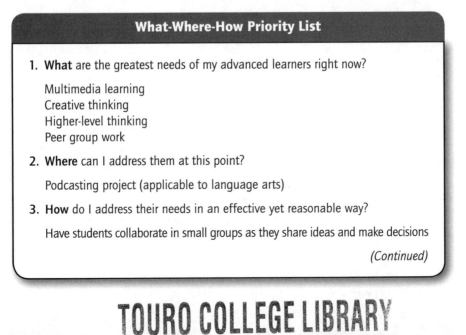

**What-Where-How Priority List**

1. **What** are the greatest needs of my advanced learners right now?

   Multimedia learning
   Creative thinking
   Higher-level thinking
   Peer group work

2. **Where** can I address them at this point?

   Podcasting project (applicable to language arts)

3. **How** do I address their needs in an effective yet reasonable way?

   Have students collaborate in small groups as they share ideas and make decisions

   *(Continued)*

(Continued)

Promote the use of higher-level thinking in conducting research and inquiry

Help students create questions for interviews

Encourage them to share arts talents (music, sound art, or voiceovers) and technical skills (editing)

Have them compose scripts for recordings

Allow skilled students to evaluate and edit podcasts

## Rationale

Podcasting provides endless possibilities for advanced students to take their learning to higher and more creative levels. Teacher Courtland Funke has used software to create monthly podcasts about his school. The project was a flexible medium for students to compose, report, write, edit, gather data, record, and so on—all higher-level thinking processes. It was largely a student-driven process with the teacher acting as adviser and moderator.

## Level

Intermediate grades and up

## Application

Any topics in the field of literature, media, history, current events, and the arts. Like an episodic radio program, the podcasts had specific themes or topics.

This is a summary of Courtland Funke's experience on doing a podcasting project (Smutny & von Fremd, 2009, pp. 59–61):

## Student Commitments

It's best if students meet once a week, preferably on a less intensive teaching day (such as Friday) when they can be excused. Alternatively, this project could work for those who test out of or otherwise prove that they can be released from instruction in a subject. Students receive homework for this podcasting project. Jobs rotate on a monthly basis, allowing everyone to work on each part of the podcast at some point.

At our first meeting, we set clearly defined jobs for the project. Each episode would feature the following:

- Two hosts
- Two producers

- Four or five writers
- A 10-question interviewer
- Composers

We later added a head writer and special reports section to the podcast.

## How It Worked

The structure for the podcast was a school news program with a short, 10-question interview segment, but students were allowed to create and add content as a group. Over the year, we added a joke of the month, student surveys, teacher surveys, reports, and news specials (art, music, gym, etc.). Writers were assigned stories to research and write as scripts for the hosts. Hosts practiced reading their scripts and recorded them for the podcast episode that month. Producers recorded each episode, edited those recordings, and inserted sound effects and music. Composers wrote and recorded music for each episode (not as hard as it sounds when using certain types of software).

## Teacher Role

As the teacher, I remained an adviser, allowing them to create ideas and ensuring that they had the time and place to do their work. However, I did steer them away from overly ambitious projects and encouraged them to think outside the box—for example, inspiring them to interview individuals beyond the school community who they felt kids would find interesting.

## Benefits

The podcasting project provided a venue for advanced students to express talents they might not ordinarily share. Musically gifted students suddenly had an outlet for composing and playing. As the project progressed, I watched students become more confident, more adventurous, and even more nurturing of one another's talents. Students who didn't think they were good writers honed their skills by writing collaboratively with stronger writers. Students who were usually timid and quiet learned to be more vocal during meetings to express their ideas to the group or to project their voices when recording their parts as hosts. I watched students take pride in their work as the months passed and grow excited each time they found a new outlet to promote the show.

### Podcasting Extensions

As mentioned in the beginning of this description, podcasting lends itself to a wide range of extensions in history, language arts, cultural studies, and the arts. Courtland Funke's process is an effective way to give students experience in creating and editing podcasts in a context (school news) that they naturally enjoy. From the skill and knowledge gained, students can use podcasting as a medium for sharing information, communicating news, or expanding peer involvement in projects or causes they care about.

### Exploring Primary and Secondary Sources

Adapted from Horn, Carol. In Smutny, J. F., & von Fremd, S. E. *Igniting Creativity in Gifted Learners, K-6: Strategies for Every Teacher.* Copyright © 2009, Corwin. pp. 100–103.

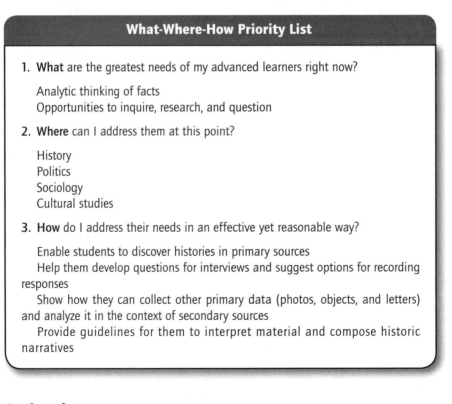

**What-Where-How Priority List**

1. **What** are the greatest needs of my advanced learners right now?

   Analytic thinking of facts
   Opportunities to inquire, research, and question

2. **Where** can I address them at this point?

   History
   Politics
   Sociology
   Cultural studies

3. **How** do I address their needs in an effective yet reasonable way?

   Enable students to discover histories in primary sources
   Help them develop questions for interviews and suggest options for recording responses
   Show how they can collect other primary data (photos, objects, and letters) and analyze it in the context of secondary sources
   Provide guidelines for them to interpret material and compose historic narratives

### Rationale

Teacher Carol Horn has found that advanced learners love *doing* history—researching primary and secondary sources to interpret the past. This approach to history places them in a more active position. Instead of assimilating facts, they examine key concepts and information, analyze their discoveries, and explore different ways of telling *their histories.*

## Level

This process can adjust to any grade.

## Application

History, geography, language arts, writing, research, analysis, and interpretation

## Description

Here is a summary of how Carol Horn guides her advanced students in making history (Smutny & von Fremd, 2009, pp. 100–103):

This process is concept-based instruction with a focus on *big ideas*, designed to engage and challenge advanced (and all) learners. When big ideas are woven throughout the curriculum, students have multiple opportunities to make connections and build on their knowledge. For students to understand how historians investigate, interpret, and re-create the past, they must focus on two unifying concepts: *discovery* and *revision.* Historians are continually searching for and discovering new clues to help them analyze and interpret the past. This is a creative enterprise where new data provides alternative views of a time or event and, therefore, new ways to understand and express it.

### Introducing Primary Sources

A good place for young historians to begin their journey of historic interpretation and analysis is through a research project that focuses on a person they know. Ralph Waldo Emerson once said, "All history becomes 'subjective; in other words, there is properly no history, only biography" (*Collected Works of Ralph Waldo Emerson—Volume II—Essays: First Series,* 2007; Smutny & von Fremd, 2009).

### A Person's Life

The study of a person's life that reaches beyond biographies and trade books can launch students on the historian's journey. By researching the life of a person they know, students gain firsthand experience in the skills a historian needs. They can draw on multiple sources of evidence using these guidelines:

*Interview.* Conduct an interview either in person, via e-mail, or on the telephone. Prepare questions ahead of time and record what you learn and what you think about the information you've gained. A copy of the interview questions, the name of the interviewee, and the date of your interview should be placed in the pocket of your research folder. Use the same process and interview at least one or more additional individuals who know this person well.

*Visit.* Plan a visit to the place where your person lives and/or works. Record what you learn along with a response in your research journal. Include photographs, postcards, or drawings of what you saw and learned. Often, you can combine a site visitation with a personal interview.

## A Focus

Students choose one aspect of this person's life that they find most interesting (childhood experiences, schooling, family event, personal success and struggle, and unusual interests and pursuits) and write a short historic narrative for a class magazine based on the evidence collected. They share their first draft with the person they're writing about to check for accuracy. They consider these questions:

1. Did you revise any ideas after you reviewed your findings, and could these findings lead to further inquiry and/or new discoveries?

2. How did your biases or preconceptions influence your understanding of this person's life?

## Doing History

By doing history through contact with a person they know, students encounter a variety of primary and secondary sources of information and begin to understand history as an ongoing process of discovery and revision. Students document their reflections in response to journal prompts and guiding questions provided by the teacher. Frequent opportunities to engage in metacognition encourage students to appreciate the power of reflection and revision as they re-create the past.

## Historic Biographies

Carol Horn's example of engaging students in history-making can extend, for advanced learners, to composing biographies.

Students first identify the reasons they chose a particular person. What do they most wish to learn? Focusing on their curiosity and interest releases them from having to follow the somewhat restrictive who-what-where-how structure of storytelling. Instead, students center research on *their* question—what is it about this person that they have to know? In other words, if they could meet him at an airport and ask one question before the person hopped on the plane, never to be seen again, what question would leap from their lips? This question emerges from other considerations: the qualities and gifts that make this a remarkable story, the challenges overcome, the hardships endured, the genesis of talent and passion, and the winding plot of turning points and pitfalls that shaped this extraordinary life.

Advanced students respond well to creative options for research and writing. Exposure to different styles of storytelling in biography—both in text and documentary form—open their minds to alternatives they might not ordinarily consider. The following is a process that advanced students have enjoyed for composing short biographies:

- **Research the big question.** Have students investigate both primary and secondary sources. Give examples of both and explore which ones most connect them to their subject. While delving into books, magazines, websites, videos, and other materials, students should seek information related to their fundamental question. They should see themselves as detectives uncovering clues. (For example, how was Rachel Carson able to summon the courage to stand up to the resistance and ridicule she faced because of her research on the damaging effects of DDT?)
- **Find clues and record discoveries.** Students choose the parts of their person's story that reveal something about their question. Selection is often the hardest part because advanced learners often find so many interesting details that they lose track of their focus. Have them record their discoveries as they read and search. These discoveries guide their writing and help them take the most significant events in their person's life and shape them into a compelling story.
- **Play with chronology.** Once students have completed their research, they can then strategize how they will reveal the answers they found to their key question. No one wants to see the punch line at the beginning of a story. Yet it can also be tedious to wade through a long chronology of a life until the story becomes interesting. Advanced students can explore alternative approaches. For example, they can start their biography in the middle of their person's life—at some turning point that will hook the reader's interest. They can write scenes down on index cards and move them around on a table or create visual displays that help them

conceptualize the shape of their story. Can they begin in the middle or end and then flash back to an earlier time? Can they find clues in Rachel Carson's childhood, for example, of the spirit and courage that she later expressed as an adult? Can they conclude their story with an event from early in the person's life that already provides hints of the person she will become?

- **Extensions.** If the students feel that their story would come alive through another medium, they can pursue other dimensions. Examples might include a free-verse poem, a collage, a graphics design, a painting, a cartoon, a dramatization, or a podcast.

Exploring primary and secondary sources in this way transforms the study of history for advanced learners. Instead of a collection of facts, history becomes an intricate crafting of stories between firsthand accounts and artifacts (primary sources) and the narratives of those who have studied them (secondary). While based on analyzing sources and meanings, history is also creative, a discovery process that reveals in every story of the past the storytellers behind it.

## Using Online Primary Sources

Adapted from Clevenson, Rhonda. In Smutny, J. F., & von Fremd, S. E. *Igniting Creativity in Gifted Learners, K-6: Strategies for Every Teacher.* Copyright © 2009, Corwin. pp. 130–136.

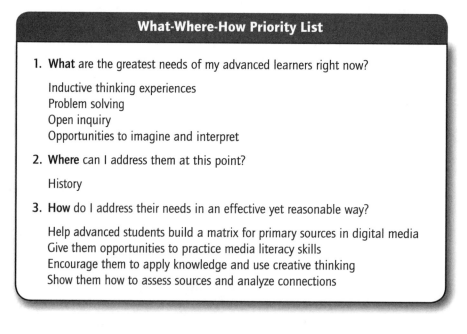

**What-Where-How Priority List**

1. **What** are the greatest needs of my advanced learners right now?

   Inductive thinking experiences
   Problem solving
   Open inquiry
   Opportunities to imagine and interpret

2. **Where** can I address them at this point?

   History

3. **How** do I address their needs in an effective yet reasonable way?

   Help advanced students build a matrix for primary sources in digital media
   Give them opportunities to practice media literacy skills
   Encourage them to apply knowledge and use creative thinking
   Show them how to assess sources and analyze connections

*Rationale for using primary sources online.* Millions of digital primary sources on the Internet invite students to become historians who use these resources to articulate history through new discoveries. This task demands a high level of literacy and critical-thinking skills. Teachers can use websites that enable them to integrate primary sources in a manageable way. The process is flexible, allowing them to gauge the appropriate level at which they integrate sources.

## Level

Intermediate to upper grades

## Application

History, geography, literacy, higher-level thinking, and research skills

## Description

For advanced learners, the opportunity to encounter and interpret images from the past ignites their imaginations as much as it challenges their thinking. The process also teaches students about the material nature of documents, photographs, maps, and other sources that they might not learn otherwise. An example is photography. Before analyzing the image itself, students need to learn that, in the field of photography, there are many techniques, formats, and styles. A teacher can significantly enhance a social studies lesson for advanced learners by integrating online photographs from the past.

*What is it?* After careful observation, the students recognize the image as that of a full-plate daguerreotype from the mid-1800s. They spend a few minutes exploring the entire picture, noting whatever details about the animate, the inanimate, and the environment that leap out at them. They write who-and-what observations (supported by specific details in the photo), and they also raise questions. After this general review, students analyze the photo one quadrant at a time, considering what they missed before, what clues they can see that tell them more about the picture. The teacher poses questions:

- What's going on in this quadrant?
- What are the people doing?
- What can you deduce from their body language, clothing, and possessions?
- What can you surmise from the environment?
- What does it say about the people or animals who live there—their social status, economic status, culture, and the like?

*How does the photographer relate to his subject?* Advanced students often love this sort of question because it invites them to look behind the scenes. "Pay no attention to that man behind the curtain!" the Wizard of Oz thundered (Fleming, 1939). What gives power to the photographic image is the wizard's (the photographer's) disappearing act. Students explore the vantage point of the photo and the choices he made in creating the image.

- Can you tell where the photographer is standing?
- What conclusions or hypotheses can you make about the photographer's relationship to the scene?
- What choices did he make in creating this image and what does that say about his attitude or feelings?

*What is the context for this image?* Advanced students can do some serious detective work in response to this question. After closely studying the image and exploring the photographer's relationship to it, they discover as much information as they can on the reason for the photograph:

- What might the occasion have been?
- Why did people take photographs like this back then?
- How did people use and understand them?
- Is there anything significant about this location and its subject that might have been considered especially important?
- What visual clues can you find that hint this?
- What sources can you consult to discover more?

Teacher Rhonda Clevenson has found a treasure trove of useful sources in the historic documents and photographs available to students online. The following is a summary of how she engages advanced learners in analyzing these sources and applying them to the study of history (Smutny & von Fremd, 2009, pp. 130–136).

### Description

Digital historic documents challenge advanced students because each source is both a puzzle by itself and one piece of the topic under study—a much larger puzzle. Teachers face major problems providing them, however. Finding the time to sift through the millions of available resources, arrange the items into meaningful groups related to the curriculum standards, and then lead students through an inquiry process is almost impossible, given the time allocated for each topic in a school day. An extraordinary website, http://www.PrimarySourceLearning.org, created by classroom teachers and sponsored by the Library of Congress Teaching With Primary Sources Northern Virginia Partnership, addresses these obstacles of search time, resource organization, and efficient inquiry routines. The website enables teachers to build on searches for digital primary sources started by other classroom teachers, create matrix groupings of primary sources based on curriculum standards, and find instructional materials that use thinking routines to guide student inquiry.

## Organizing Primary Sources Into a Matrix

Through this website, advanced students can compare two primary sources or use a small group of them to corroborate ideas presented in a textbook or discovered through research in the classroom. These useful strategies can be even more effective when the teacher asks students to organize the sources into a matrix or table. The horizontal rows might represent different types of facts or concepts that students must know for standardized tests, and the vertical rows might represent themes, persons, places, or periods. The matrix as a whole—considering both the vertical and horizontal columns—challenges students to consider a large-scale idea that is central to the discipline. The matrix may also be used to structure the process of writing research papers by asking students to support their thesis with evidence from the images in a row or column. When students build a matrix instead of putting resources in a group, they use creative thinking, apply knowledge, and practice media literacy skills to determine which source is the best fit for a topic and for the connections and patterns suggested by other sources.

## Inquiry Routines

Students choose one source from the matrix to examine carefully through an inquiry process. An inquiry process teaches students to resist the impulse to draw hasty conclusions and to allow more time for thoughtful exploration. Students often begin with describing the composition, content, bibliographic information, and possible purpose of the primary source. They then use background knowledge to connect this information to its historical context, leading them to make inferences and observations. Here is a three-step process:

1. The first impulse that learners have when looking at a primary source is to connect what they see to previous experiences. This

process of making connections to previous knowledge is one of the most important factors in building understanding.

2. Next, learners examine the source closely and ask questions: What do I know about this source? What don't I know about this source? How can I find out more about this source?

3. Last, students apply the source to their study of a topic. They consider further questions: What might this source tell me about the topic? How might this source confirm, challenge, or change my thinking? The students select an image and analyze it through their knowledge and experience. They continue to expand and reinterpret their understanding of their topic, raising research questions they'd like to pursue in the future.

Primary sources are fragments of life that survived. Whether the source is a picture, letter, map, sound recording, or oral history, the source does not come with a single interpretation. For advanced learners, the benefits of using them in the classroom are immediate. Curiosity rises exponentially as they apply themselves to real-life puzzles, questioning, reflecting, and making new connections.

*Creative extensions.* When students make direct contact with primary sources—online or not—they feel transported to another place and time. We have all felt this. Standing in front of an exhibit on Abraham Lincoln—seeing an old pair of spectacles or reading a letter he wrote in his own handwriting—summon the man like no biography possibly can. Teachers can engage the imaginations of advanced students through creative extensions. They can write free-verse poems, conjure imagined scenes, interviews, or stories through dramatizations, and create artistic designs, collages, or paintings. All of these enrich students' imaginative engagement with primary sources.

You can use ideas from any of the teaching activities just described not only for advanced but for all students, adjusting the process or materials as needed. Some of the descriptions may seem too extensive for the time and resources you have. Bear in mind, though, that most teachers attempt new ideas on a small scale first, expanding them only as they become more practiced. To assist you further, we've included two charts that offer examples of how you can adapt lesson plans (or parts of lesson plans) in workable ways. The charts include both low-preparation and high-preparation strategies, and they are intended only as a reference.

*Language Arts*

| Learning Needs | High-Preparation Strategies | Low-Preparation Strategies |
|---|---|---|
| Fast readers Higher-level thinkers Skilled writers | **Tiered Instruction**<br><br>Tier 1: Students read a short story, and then summarize in a paragraph the most important moment in the story and why.<br><br>Tier 2: They read a more difficult story, analyze how the author uses point of view in the story, and hypothesize how the story might have turned out through another character's point of view. | **Change Sources**<br><br>Students do the same assignment but use a novel instead of a story (or a more difficult story).<br><br>**Change Thinking Process**<br><br>They use the same story but require higher-level thinking—comparison, analysis, imagination. |
| Strong Interests Reading and writing Connections to real world | **Interest Centers**<br><br>In a unit on biography, students explore the story of the Wright brothers' historic flight at a center on inventions and create posters with text and art.<br><br>In a unit on poetry, they go to a center to read poems they love, select visual catalysts (pictures, photos, etc.) to write free-verse poems. | **Extension Activities**<br><br>Students compose letters to the editor of a local newspaper to address a local issue.<br><br>They research the historic period of Emily Dickinson's New England to understand her poems in a broader context. |
| Visual and kinesthetic learning preferences Creative media | **Arts Integration**<br><br>Students use the visual and performing arts throughout the learning experience. | **Choices in Sources and Processes**<br><br>Students create collage-poems by combining images, |

*(Continued)*

(Continued)

| Learning Needs | High-Preparation Strategies | Low-Preparation Strategies |
|---|---|---|
| | They do a reader's theater production to demonstrate their understanding of story structure. | shapes, and colors with lines of text).<br><br>They do a radio recording as a journalist reporting on an incident in their neighborhood. |
| Immersion study In-depth inquiry Interdisciplinary | **Independent Study**<br><br>Students choose topics of interest, and, together with the teacher, design their projects (timeline, goals, etc.). For example, they explore different sections of local newspapers and create a newspaper using pictures, drawings, and cartoons. | **Simpler Explorations**<br><br>Students record weather conditions and create weather reports (with diagrams and sketches).<br><br>They research the history of the Asian Longhorned Beetle and how it came to the United States. They write a report on the strategies used to stop it and speculate about the results of these efforts. |

*Social Studies*

| Learning Needs | High-Preparation Strategies | Low-Preparation Strategies |
|---|---|---|
| Fast readers Higher-level thinkers Skilled writers | **Tiered Instruction**<br><br>Tier 1: Students watch a video about Ellis Island and create a picture journal of an immigrant story.<br><br>Tier 2: They read firsthand stories of those who came through Ellis Island, and | **Change Sources**<br><br>Students use more difficult texts, multimedia, hands-on materials, and Internet sites.<br><br>**Change Thinking Process**<br><br>They analyze the main causes of immigration to the |

| Learning Needs | High-Preparation Strategies | Low-Preparation Strategies |
|---|---|---|
| | search the Internet; they assume the identity of specific travelers and write memoirs of their experiences—why they left home, their struggles, and their hopes and dreams. | United States and what foreign countries produced the most immigrants in a particular period. |
| **Strong Interests**<br><br>Culture<br>Map-making<br>Current events<br>Connections to real-world issues and problems | **Interest Centers**<br><br>Students use centers that create many points of entry to a subject. A social studies center could provide books, magazines, writing prompts, visual materials like maps and historic prints, and activities cards that connect to *student interests*. For example, in a unit on the settlement of the Great Lakes region, children could research the Potawatomi Nation, whose word "Chicagou" became Chicago. They could write poems, stories, essays on their lives before Whites came and create a poster with a map and artwork. | **Extension Activities**<br><br>Students draw on personal interests to extend an assignment—either by exploring a related issue or by advancing their study to a higher level. For example, in a unit on Native Americans in the Great Lakes, students extend their reports by doing an Internet search of the legends of Nanabozho (a mythic hero and trickster) and create an original version of one of the stories. |
| Visual and kinesthetic learning preferences<br>Creative media | **Arts Integration**<br><br>Students engage in an arts process that assumes a major part of the unit. For example, in a study of early settlers in their state, students collect and perform the personal narratives of these new | **Choices in Sources and Processes**<br><br>Students choose more challenging assignments by substituting a source (more sophisticated book, technology, or diagram) or process (spatial reasoning, analysis). For example, in a |

*(Continued)*

(Continued)

| Learning Needs | High-Preparation Strategies | Low-Preparation Strategies |
|---|---|---|
| | arrivals through a reader's theater process. They intersperse these stories with historic reports that provide a context for their lives. | unit on the golden age of aviation, they examine the impact of Lindbergh's Atlantic flight of 1927on public perception of the possibilities of travel. |
| Immersion study In-depth inquiry Interdisciplinary | **Independent Study** Students undertake an extensive project ensuring maximum depth and providing less time constraints. For example, they explore different sections of local newspapers and create a newspaper, using photographs, drawing, and cartoons. | **Simpler Explorations** Students choose a quote from a famous historic figure, trace it back in time, and express what they discovered through writing, drama, or art. Alternative: They share the quote with people in their lives, record their responses to it, and compare these to the original source of the quote. |

## PARTING THOUGHTS FOR YOUR JOURNEY

*Introduce critical thinking in popular sources.* Students are bombarded with information, images, reports, sound bites, and rumors posing as news. They text messages back and forth, check e-mail, share links and Facebook entries, often without questioning what they see or hear. Students need to develop a more critical eye and awareness of the influences behind the information. Both language arts and social studies offer ways to examine text and image sources with questions such as these: Who composed this? What were their sources, and how reliable were/are they? What is the purpose or hidden message of the report, blog, or image? Is there a bias or assumption that they can see? Students love exploring their sources of information, and these kinds of questions provide a connection to the curriculum and help them think more critically about media-generated reports.

*Make biographies a dimension of the classroom environment.* Biography belongs in every subject. Behind every scientific discovery, historic artifact, novel, map, and artwork are the life stories of pioneers who rarely make their appearance in the curriculum. Students often learn concepts and facts as though they sprang spontaneously out of the Earth—a situation that makes them less engaged or curious. What restores meaning to subjects are the stories of those whose lifework yielded the discoveries and innovations that we now accept as knowledge.

In every unit, consider how you can integrate the contributions of historic figures, poets, artists, musicians, geographers, mathematicians, scientists, and so forth. As shared earlier in this chapter, the process of writing, sketching, and designing biographical exhibits can become a tool for students to connect to any unit. A teacher we know devotes part of a wall to biographies written and illustrated by his students. He calls it the biographical hall of fame, and it adds inspiration and meaning to any topic the class is studying.

*Find new uses for poetry and song.* Students of all ability levels come to love poetry when introduced to contemporary poems they can relate to and when given time to develop their own. Raps are poems, as are popular songs (though not all of them would qualify). Capitalize on students' play with language by treating poetry less like a fine art reserved for the poet and more like a versatile and accessible medium open to anyone who has something to say. Share recordings of "spoken word" poetry—a style of verse (often politically charged, socially relevant, passionate, or autobiographical) intended to be performed (rather than written) and characteristic of the work shared at many popular poetry slams. Create time for students to share and/or perform poems they've found as well as those they've composed. Invite a spoken-word poet to perform his work and share how poetry has become a creative medium for him to give voice to his life stories. Reading and sharing poems opens the imaginations of students. Like biographies, poems assume a life of their own, giving advanced learners the space they need to express their thoughts and feelings in ways they rarely can in any other medium.

# Teaching Advanced Students in Science and Mathematics

**F**or many students, the scientific and mathematical worlds begin as a nature experience. They observe a monarch butterfly feeding on the milk thistle, touch the hanging beard moss, listen to the song of the hermit thrush, and calculate the time it takes a centipede to reach the top of a fern. They *want to know* what things are made of and how to understand them—how, for example, to identify species of birds by shape, behavior, and habitat. Without discovery, science and math have little chance of inspiring interest in the physical world. The "why" questions that impel children through their earliest years of life should become catalysts for teaching in the classroom. Curiosity is a powerful motivator for students, guiding them to draw on what they know to ask deeper questions, test, experiment, observe, and share their discoveries. All of this puts them in the process of *doing* science and math as well as learning about it.

In the areas of thinking and skill development, mathematics involves similar processes as those used in science. A growing priority in both science and math instruction is to give students real-world experience with the puzzles and problems they might encounter and to help them strategize solutions. In science, they explore systems, organizations, phenomena of change and constancy, and biological forms and functions. They observe, classify, make inferences, predict, measure, use numbers, create models, identify variables, formulate hypotheses, record and interpret data, and draw conclusions. In mathematics, students focus on numbers and operations, algebra, geometry, measurement, data analysis, and probability. As in the study of science, they analyze what they know, reason inductively and deductively, design models, evaluate their thinking process, investigate problems, predict outcomes, and verify solutions.

Advanced students typically need more in both math and science instruction than learning additional content. As we've explored in this book already, compacting the curriculum—allowing students to eliminate unnecessary review and practice—is a positive choice for those who know more than their peers. But the question is, What do they do with the time they've gained? Sometimes, students can move on to more advanced content, perhaps even attend classes in a higher grade. However, in many cases, what they most need is a different kind of learning experience, ideally, an open-ended problem or puzzle related to the unit that allows more than one approach to solve it.

Think about the following eight suggestions, offered by a sixth-grade math teacher, on how to connect advanced students to the mystery and wonder of exploring and solving new problems (Freeman, 2003, pp. 74–76).

1. Give students the opportunity to think inductively.
   Too often, students learn the theories or formulas and then spend time applying them to predefined problems. Advanced thinkers quickly get bored with this. They need the chance to discover the process or formula operating in a math or science situation. Designing these opportunities can produce unexpected results, as some creative students always seem to find a way you hadn't anticipated.

2. Avoid compressing content into short time.
   Though we all have to resort to presenting the theories or concepts to our students some of the time, it's important to offer opportunities for advanced students to *discover* something new, whether this be a pattern, a relationship, a process, or concept they hadn't seen before. The detective work of math (or science) is lost when students spend too much time committing to memory what former mathematicians have accomplished.

3. Allow students time to explore and make discoveries.
   There are different ways to do this. You can present an idea to the whole class and set up a challenge for them to investigate as a

whole group. Or they can work individually, in pairs, or in trios. As students present their discoveries, you can pose questions, point out a pertinent fact or two, and suggest another approach. Having students verify or dispute one another's proposals also expands the process.

4. Keep the activities open-ended.
   Help students brainstorm the different possibilities. Encourage unexpected responses. Use questioning to follow up on student ideas and suggest other approaches. Encourage peer sharing when students are stuck or feel they've reached a dead end.

5. Avoid contrived and artificial problems.
   Of course, sometimes you have to impart content as clearly and directly as possible, checking their understanding through pre-arranged exercises or tests. However, whenever possible, formulate problems that have some interest and relevance, where students can see, "Yes, without understanding air pressure, we wouldn't have a barometer and be able to calculate changes in the weather."

6. Avoid repeating the regular curriculum.
   Enrichment activities should relate to the curriculum but not repeat it. You don't want to set up advanced students for more boredom by giving them content already planned for the months ahead. Draw from the concepts they're learning and provide opportunities for them to apply them to interesting situations that demand higher-level thinking and reasoning.

7. Do not grade.
   If you have to grade, make it clear to them that you will record whether they participate, try their best, take risks, not whether they get a "right" answer. Otherwise, students will confine themselves to safe, low-risk choices and never use their potential for more imaginative responses.

8. Ensure that topics are mathematically (or scientifically) significant.
   Advanced students are immediately intrigued by topics that are central to the study of math or science. Both science and math are active *doing* fields that involve specific processes (observation, comparison, and application) and specific modes of thinking (logical, analytical, and imaginative). With Internet access,

teachers today can find many excellent options for integrating topics related to the curriculum. (See the Resource for links that can help you get started.)

---

Adapted from Freeman, Christopher M. *Designing Math Curriculum to Encourage Inductive Thinking by Elementary and Middle School Students: Basic Principles to Follow.* In Smutny, J. F. *Designing and Developing Programs for Gifted Students.* Copyright © 2002, Corwin. pp. 74–76.

As with the previous chapter, this one also includes examples from classroom teachers of ideas they've found beneficial for advanced students in science and math. Consider again the priority list as you plan alternative activities.

---

### What-Where-How Priority List

1. **What** are the greatest needs of my advanced learners right now?

**Identify needs, interests, and learning styles**

K-W-L charts
Assignments
Tests
Talent days
Observation
Feedback (parents or other school personnel)

2. **Where** can I address them at this point?

**Focus on big ideas, concepts, and skills**

Science
Skills (observation, application, testing, and experimentation)
Thinking (induction, deduction, inquiry, and analysis)
Mathematics
Skills (calculation, measurement, and hand-eye coordination)
Thinking (induction, deduction, problem solving, and analysis)

3. **How** do I address their needs in an effective yet reasonable way?

**Create choices with challenge**

Faster pace
Higher-level thinking (taxonomies)
Creative thinking
The arts
Grouping/pairs
Independent learning

When you look at your lesson plans in math and science for the next week or two, what do you see as the greatest needs of your advanced students? K-W-L charts can clarify the areas where students excel and need more challenge. Otherwise, prior assignments, tests, and careful observation can help you identify those who need changes and where they need them. Be open to feedback from parents. Consulting with them can yield helpful information on students' interests, and you may be able to incorporate these into a unit you're already teaching. Enabling students to share their experiences enriches the classroom and helps you to tap into what motivates and inspires them.

As in the previous chapter, teachers try to organize their units around big ideas and fundamental skills that reflect the standards and learning benchmarks in each subject area.

---

### Focus on Essentials

#### Level I: Essential Themes, Concepts, and Principles

- A single, broad question

#### Examples

What does "species" actually mean?
How does a "species" relate to a "class?"
How do scientists classify animals?

#### Level II: Information, Concepts, and Skills Tied to Learning Standards

- A few, student-centered questions

#### Examples

What bird species can you identify in your neighborhood?

What key physical characteristics distinguish one species from another (e.g., size, color, markings, shape of beak, flight pattern, etc.)?

How can habitat help you identify a bird species (water, desert, scrub, prairie, forest, urban/suburban)?

---

The focus on essentials gives you the flexibility to modify assignments for advanced students. Some teachers present an open question about some math or science puzzle as a regular part of the week's activities. Exploring a curious phenomenon apart from regular schoolwork can prompt students to raise the very questions a teacher wants to explore during the week. Its spontaneous appearance and lack of introduction make it more interesting. A teacher begins the week's science or math unit not with an overview or introduction but with a question. "What do you think is causing the invasion of giant squid off the California coast?" She writes it on the board, and students take turns offering possible theories. A few agree to do some digging and return the next day with some ideas; the next day, students share their research, which often spawns more questions. By now, the class is hooked. A "curiosity of the week" takes little class time and gives advanced students the freedom to share their passions and talents apart from the regular curriculum. As the year progresses, more students start bringing in their curious questions for the class to ponder. Through this and other practices, science and math become what they are—rich and virtually unlimited worlds of surprising facts and unsolved mysteries.

As you consider what to do for these students, think about the resources you have and the kind of thinking processes in science and math that will best promote their abilities and growth. This chapter assumes that some weeks allow a little more time than others in which to plan and integrate alternative learning experiences for advanced students. The charts at the end of this chapter provide examples of different activities—some requiring less preparation than others—so that you can keep responding to these students, whatever the circumstances of your day or week.

Next are some examples used by teachers we know that illustrate how to create more challenging choices for advanced students. They're included only to inspire your ideas. As in the previous chapter, consider the elements first described in Chapter 3 and how you might incorporate them into your units:

- Choices provided for advanced students in assignments or projects
- Accelerated learning incorporated for fast learners
- Creative process and use of the arts integrated wherever possible
- Student interests emphasized
- Peer collaboration in group projects encouraged where appropriate
- Technology incorporated
- Independent learning allowed
- Self-assessment skills taught to monitor progress

## EXAMPLES

Adapted from Fayer, Liz. In Smutny, J. F., von Fremd, S. E. *Igniting Creativity in Gifted Learners, K-6: Strategies for Every Teacher*. Copyright 2009, Corwin, pp. 162–164.

### Problem-Based Learning in Science

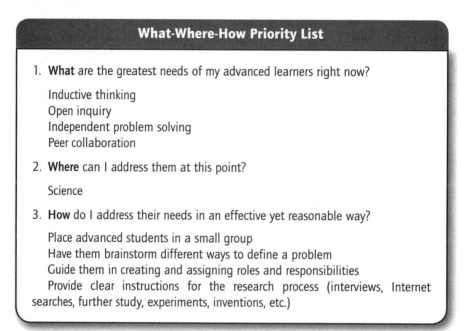

**What-Where-How Priority List**

1. **What** are the greatest needs of my advanced learners right now?

   Inductive thinking
   Open inquiry
   Independent problem solving
   Peer collaboration

2. **Where** can I address them at this point?

   Science

3. **How** do I address their needs in an effective yet reasonable way?

   Place advanced students in a small group
   Have them brainstorm different ways to define a problem
   Guide them in creating and assigning roles and responsibilities
   Provide clear instructions for the research process (interviews, Internet searches, further study, experiments, inventions, etc.)

### Rationale

Problem-based learning (PBL) is a highly effective way for advanced students to experience the creative dimension of science and to participate actively in tackling a real-world problem. At each step, they engage in a number of scientific processes: observation, exploration, data analysis, experimentation, hypothesizing and creative thinking.

### Level

All grades

### Application

Science, research and inquiry, math, literacy

### Description

At a most basic level, PBL examines a phenomenon or problem and asks the following questions: (1) What do we know? (2) What do we need to know? (3) How can we find out?

Because of the inquiring nature of science and the emphasis on exploration and creative thinking that PBL offers, advanced students quickly respond to the challenge. The best way for students to learn science is to *experience* problems that are ill defined. In other words, they encounter a situation or problem that they want to understand. Only by understanding something about it can they take the progressive steps—often unknown to them at the start—to achieve it. A key idea in PBL is that students encounter problems that are as ill defined as they are in real situations encountered by scientists. This is in contrast to traditional science teaching where students address problems *after* they've already learned the information they need to solve it. This gives students the misapprehension that any problem they find in math or science will be one where they possess all the necessary skills and information. For advanced students, this is an ideal context for learning because it not only asks what the nature of a problem is and what they don't know but also what knowledge base, skills, and approaches could be of use that they're unaware of? In other words, what do I need to know and what do I need to know that I don't know I need to know? Often, the process of defining a problem and exploring its solution unearths other areas where they need more information or understanding.

This summary is of the sequence fifth-grade teacher Liz Fayer followed in a weather unit (Smutny & von Fremd, 2009, pp. 162–164):

*Knowledge level.* After preassessing the students, she realized that they needed additional knowledge to make informed decisions during the beginning of the PBL process. Through demonstrations, experiments, research, and newscasts about weather, she provided background knowledge and experience that better prepared them for the kinds of questions they would be exploring in PBL.

*The ill-defined problem.* The teacher knew that the students needed to encounter a real-life problem related to the subject of weather. She then presented the schedule for the outdoor education day to be held at the end of the year. What might the impact of local weather be on the scheduled day? What, if anything, can be done? Although the students could find weather predictions on the Internet for their suburb, they could not find them for their school. As they brainstormed, they explored different ways to understand and define the nature of their problem.

*The question.* In facing any problem, it's important for students to ask themselves the following questions: What about this problem is interesting? What's the real challenge presented by this problem? What do we need to find out? As brainstorming ensued, students posed their ill-structured question, "How can we predict the weather for our school for outdoor education day?" Establishing the question set the PBL in motion. Students took turns leading small groups in discussions about weather prediction. What does weather prediction involve? What are the steps? What information do we need? How precise is it? The teacher offered guiding questions, suggested options for students to consider, and guided the management of groups.

*Planning and strategizing.* To help the students strategize, teachers could ask, What is your plan? How will you organize yourselves so that everyone is responsible for his piece? How will you communicate with one another about what you're finding and what else you need to do? Follow-up questions might include these: Since you have decided to interview people, *who* will you interview? Who will analyze the data you collect from weather equipment and/or reports and statistics that you find? How will you record this?

*Authentic outcome.* Fayer's students studied the weather in their area by exploring cloudscapes, creating weather stations, inventing and building weather equipment, collecting and analyzing data, predicting, and then evaluating how accurate their predictions were (with respect to the outdoor education day). Because this educational experience led to an authentic outcome they cared about, students expressed a high level of critical thinking and self-directedness throughout the process.

Advanced students love tackling real problems. Who has not seen the odd invention of a child determined to create a new trapdoor for a treasured pet? Or a child determined to build a new contraption for trapping pesky houseflies in the summer? Students' personal investment and interest in a problem motivate them to solve it. Fayer described the impact that student invention had on the PBL process (Smutny & von Fremd, 2009, p. 164). Of particular note is the fact that her advanced students chose not to consult the Internet to guide their creative process. She explains it in this way:

> *Student invention.* "One interesting point to share is that while the gifted students may have used the Internet to research weather equipment, and they could have chosen to build it the way the directions dictated, they often choose their own route. A fascinating piece of equipment that was built by gifted students was an anemometer (an instrument for measuring wind speed). Although there are many interesting designs on the Internet, this group chose not to look, and instead designed their own. They used a tube that was one meter long, a timer, and cotton balls. When they went outside to measure the wind, they held the cotton ball at one end and as they let it go in the direction the wind was blowing, they started the timer. They determined that the wind speed was $X$ number of meters per second. Incredibly simple and incredibly inventive!"

This description is a brief outline of how one teacher used PBL to open a class science process for advanced students. Often, PBL also involves sharing the results of their discoveries and examining how well the findings help students understand the problem. These findings also lead to an inquiry into more creative solutions to be discussed, examined, tested, and explored.

## Rain Forest

Adapted from Whitman, Rachel. In Smutny, J. F., & von Fremd, S. E. *Igniting Creativity in Gifted Learners, K–6: Strategies for Every Teacher.* Copyright © 2009, Corwin. pp. 184–187.

---

### What-Where-How Priority List

1. **What** are the greatest needs of my advanced learners right now?

   Immersion experience
   Discovery
   Outlet for imagination and creative expression

2. **Where** can I address them at this point?

   Science

3. **How** do I address their needs in an effective yet reasonable way?

   Have them participate in designing and building a rain forest
   Provide sources for them to research a layer of the forest, raise questions, and explore animal and plant life
   Guide them in handling the elements of the forest themselves and in analyzing the complex interrelationships

---

## Rationale

Young advanced learners discover the life and ecology of a rain forest by creating the environment layer by layer. This explorative process draws on inquiry, discussion, and imaginative and artistic expression. It provides a kinesthetic way for students to learn about and appreciate the extraordinary biodiversity of tropical rain forests.

## Level

Primary grades

## Application

Science, art, construction, literacy

## Description

Tropical rain forests are more biologically diverse than any other eco-system on Earth. Students are often awed by the sheer scope of this diversity: an estimated 10 million species thriving in the remaining habitat, with only 1.4 million actually named. The very notion that millions of species remain undiscovered and unstudied breaks the illusion of science as a monolithic, self-contained field of knowledge to be acquired incrementally year after year. The world of science is one of ongoing discovery, one that involves continuous research, testing, and observation to understand the behaviors of toucans or howler monkeys and of the complex ecology of plants and insects on the forest floor. Creating a rain forest habitat enables advanced students to learn by discovery—by building the different layers and doing their own inquiries into the plant and animal life in each layer.

Primary teacher Rachel Whitman structures her rain forest unit around two foci:

Focus 1: The layers of the rain forest

Focus 2: The animal life in the various layers of the rain forest

This is a summary of Rachel Whitman's discovery approach to teaching about the rain forest (Smutny & von Fremd, 2009, pp. 184–187):

## Focus 1: Layers of the Forest

*Step 1.* The teacher begins with book exploration to build background knowledge and to enhance the understanding of those who have had some exposure to the topic. This ensures that all students have a baseline of information to participate in the project. Whitman recommends at least 20 or more nonfiction books for a class of 15. The books should contain pictures, particularly for the early primary students. The floor is an ideal place for students to thumb through the books, as younger children love to spread out while they read, study the pictures, and share with one another. Prior to this process, the teacher poses open questions about the rain forest as a way of gauging what they know (the K-W-L chart is useful here). Some teachers have also used audio recordings of rain forests that evoke all sorts of questions, sensations, and imaginative images in students' minds.

At the end of the book exploring period (a 20- to 30-minute process), the teacher gathers her students back together to discuss what they learned. As the children report their findings, she writes them down on a chart or poster board.

*Step 2.* Step 2 begins with introducing the topic: the four layers of the rain forest. As the class discusses each layer, the teacher draws a picture/symbol for it, and then writes the name down. Students soon become comfortable in this communal environment, where they can contribute what they've discovered or pose questions about the different layers. Once the students achieve some conceptual understanding of the layers, the teacher breaks the class into smaller groups. Each one gathers around a pile of books divided into four categories: (1) forest floor, (2) understory, (3) canopy, and (4) emergent layer. As the groups explore each layer, they describe what they learned and saw in the books. After five to seven minutes, the groups switch until the students have explored all layers.

*Step 3.* At Step 3, the teacher assigns each group a layer of the rain forest. The students recognize their layer from the symbol or word she makes on the chart, and this saves the teacher from having to remind them where they belong; they can look at the chart and see their name printed in the group.

Each group constructs their assigned layer of the rain forest. Giant leaf templates represent a layer. Whitman found it fairly simple to arrange students into groups once they have their assigned leaves. Each group has a particular set of materials, supplies, and directions—all set out in the prearranged groupings. As the class gathers around on the floor, the teacher holds up the forest floor layer and explains how to trace the leaf, cut it out, and paint it. She then asks the members of that group to stand, take their trace templates, and walk to their work area with their group. She then repeats these directions for the remaining layers. Eventually, the room is buzzing with everyone building his or her layer of the rain forest.

Over the course of the next several days, the teacher collects the layers and hangs them on a tent frame. Whitman uses shipping tape to place the forest floor layers down and keep them anchored there. With shipping tape, the teacher can also attach the understory and canopy layers, while using sticks to elevate the emergent layer above the tent frame. The final step in this process is to make vines. The teacher models for the class how to make their vines from a paper grocery bag: Cut up one narrow side, and then cut away the bottom of the bag, leaving one giant rectangle; twist the rectangle until it looks like a vine. Each child repeats this step with a second bag. Finally, the class tapes the bags together to make multiple long vines.

### Focus 2: Animal Life in Forest Layers

*Step 4.* Similar to Step 1, students explore books again (perhaps this time, in the rain forest). Teachers have included a variety of resources in this kind of exploration: video footage, Internet sites with pictures and scientific information on animal species at different levels, games, and audio recordings. The focus of this step is to discover rain forest animals. After the kids explore various sources, they discuss the animals they found and the teacher writes them on the poster board. They respond to the question, What animals do we see in the emergent, canopy, understory, and forest floor?

*Step 5.* If needed, the teacher has students return to their sources to explore new questions and understand better where animals spend most of their lives and why. What sources of food exist in the canopy and what other physical needs of animals does this layer provide for? What layer do the predators live in and why? Where do the insects prefer to be? These and other questions prompt students to revisit sources and seek new ones as they follow new lines of inquiry.

*Step 6.* The teacher then assigns groups to make particular animals for the layers. For example, birds for the emergent, frogs for the forest floor, snakes for the understory, and monkeys for the canopy. Some teachers involve their art colleagues in this process. Students paint, do collage, and construct shapes from a variety of materials.

This kind of process lays the foundation for advanced learners to engage in higher-level thinking and to explore topics and issues far beyond their present understanding. Creating a habitat from the ground up prompts questions about rain forest ecology and about the complex relationships between species.

### Extensions

A unit such as this provides a host of extensions activities for advanced students. Examples could include the following:

- A more in-depth study of a rain forest animal, including its present status as a creature in a shrinking habitat
- A poem about a part of the forest or an animal species
- A mural (group activity)

In our experience, we have found that students love to place themselves imaginatively in the body of an animal. Students could write, sketch, or narrate a day in the life of a tapir, a squirrel monkey, an iguana, or a toucan. Consider the extraordinary life of the green basilisk, a lizard that spends much of its time in the trees but never far from a body of water. It has specially designed feet that enable it to run across water without sinking. When threatened, it drops from a tree into the water and sprints about five feet per second across the surface. After a while, gravity eventually weighs them down, but the basilisk merely shifts its mode of transportation to its equally dazzling swimming skills. Such extensions, provided whenever a student has completed his assigned work, enable advanced learners to take their learning to a larger, more creative level.

## Solar Power

---

### What-Where-How Priority List

1. **What** are the greatest needs of my advanced learners right now?

   Hands-on process
   Experimenting, exploring
   Sharing with peers

2. **Where** can I address them at this point?

   Science
   Mathematics

3. **How** do I address their needs in an effective yet reasonable way?

   Provide opportunities for them to make careful observations of an object or process
   Encourage them to discuss questions and make suggestions
   Invite them to explore data, analyze evidence, and present hypotheses
   Guide them in creating experiments, making diagrams, and building solar ovens

---

## Rationale

Solar power is the conversion of sunlight into electricity. This fact alone means that for students, the science involved will not be an isolated discipline focused on facts, figures, and abstract content. A natural phenomenon—the sun—is being harnessed for practical use on Earth. Advanced students find in the study of solar power a new arena for them to explore phenomena, raise questions, make predictions, observe results, and experiment with what they have learned.

## Level

Primary to intermediate grades, adaptable to higher grades

## Application

Solar power applies to a wide range of subject areas—reading, writing, mathematics, the arts, and more. Teachers can extract and modify segments of this instruction to enhance their curriculum for advanced students. They can also apply the strategies to other interdisciplinary learning experiences in science.

Teacher Carol Howe uses the concept of solar power to open the science curriculum for advanced students. She begins with an introductory activity that motivates the class to observe a mysterious object and puzzle over its purpose. This arouses their curiosity and engages their interest from the start. As science detectives, they have to ask relevant questions and look for clues. Here is a summary of her process (Smutny & von Fremd, 2009, pp. 170–177).

## Introduce Scientific Process Through a Mystery Object

1. *Observe.* Students go to a table, handle/examine the mystery object (a photon ball), and write what they observe about it.

2. *Ask questions.* What do I think this object is? What does it look like? How does it feel when I touch it? Does it make any sound? What does it do? Is it alive? Is it a machine? What makes it run?

3. *Make a prediction.* Students offer their ideas on what the object is and substantiate their claims with evidence and logical arguments.

4. *Investigate/measure/explore.* After discussing student predictions—testing, observing, and asking further questions—students reach a consensus on the object.

5. *Write/draw conclusions.* Students record the results of their investigation, citing specific evidence that proves the reliability of their conclusions.

## Journal Comments by Carol Howe

The mystery object amused students. They shared observations and questions after being prompted how to do an experiment and investigation, writing what they observed. They learned how essential it is to use the five senses and the five Ws (who, what, where, when, and why); plus, one student added, "How?" when observing. Sample student observations included noting that the mystery object is plastic; round with strange, colorful bumps (possibly antennae); makes strange noises; blinks different colored lights; vibrates (shakes); rolls across the table; stops and starts at will, and bounces.

## What Is Energy? What Are Some Types of Energy?

### Hands-On Activity

- The teacher creates a series of stations for the students to explore energy—one for each type (e.g., light, mechanical, electric, and solar).
- Students visit each station with a clipboard and record K-W-L observations—what they *know*, what they *want* to know, and what they need to *learn*. Howe created the following chart as a guide for this activity:

| Energy Station (What We Know) | Where Does the Energy Come From? (What We Want to Know) | How Do You Know It Has Energy? (What We Need to Learn) |
|---|---|---|
| Windup toy | Mechanical/machine | Toy moves |
| Solar-powered car, fan, radio, and lightbulb (items have solar cells to absorb light) | Solar energy cells absorb light and convert to energy | Car moves, radio plays, bulb lights, fan turns |
| Electric object (plug-in lamp) | Plug-in lamp | Lamp lights |
| Electric blanket | Plug device into electric wall socket | Coils get warm |
| Radiometer | Housed in a glass ball, the white and black panels absorb light and heat at different temperatures, making the panels turn in a circle | White and black panels spin in circles |

*(Continued)*

(Continued)

| Energy Station (What We Know) | Where Does the Energy Come From? (What We Want to Know) | How Do You Know It Has Energy? (What We Need to Learn) |
|---|---|---|
| Kinetic silver balls | Silver balls suspended on nylon strings that keep colliding as they bounce off one another | Silver balls bounce against one another; perpetual energy comes from bouncing against one another |
| Sound-tuning fork, drums | Vibrates and gives off sound when struck | A humming sound; a drum rat-a-tat sound |

### Journal Comments by Carol Howe

Students had a great time examining the windup toy (mechanical), solar car, solar-powered fan, light, electric blanket, lightbulb, heat element, radiometer, solar calculator, and pinwheels. Students drew wonderful diagrams of each type of energy. Students were amazed that someday, much of the world will be powered by solar energy to replace the need for oil. Students concluded the following:

- Energy is all around us in many forms.
- Energy is the ability to do work (move) or the ability to make things change.
- Energy cannot disappear. It can only change into other forms of energy; for example, light energy can change into heat energy.

### What Are Some Practical Uses for Solar Energy?

*Hands-On Activity*

Advanced students love learning about new sources of energy, but applying this knowledge to a result that pleases their taste buds cannot fail to motivate them. Carol Howe has taught primary students how to construct a solar oven from a pizza box. After building the oven, they test its workability by cooking s'mores with it and observing closely how solar energy (light and heat) can be sufficiently harnessed to efficiently power everyday home appliances.

*Making a Solar Oven*

These are the materials required:

| | |
|---|---|
| Thin cardboard box (pizza box) | Scissors |
| Black construction paper | Exacto knife |
| Aluminum foil | Two graham cracker squares |
| Clear transparency | Six small marshmallows |
| Tape | One-third chocolate bar per student |
| Glue | |

1. The first step in this process is to direct students to glue aluminum foil to the three-sided lid in the top of the cardboard box. The teacher raises questions: How do we harness the sun's energy for our ovens? What property in aluminum foil might aid in conducting heat? As they work and share ideas, the students realize that the foil reflects the sun's light toward the bottom of the cardboard box, where the s'mores will be.

2. Next, they cut a square hole in the top of the box and attach a piece of transparency to cover the square hole in the top of the box. Again, the teacher can raise questions according to the student's age and level of understanding. Clearly, the hole allows sunlight to pass through. But where does it go from there? How can this heat source be increased to heat the bottom of the box and melt the s'mores?

3. Some students may already know the last step by observing the supplies and thinking about their uses. The teacher can ask, If the aluminum foil reflects light, what will absorb it, and how do you know this? The students then glue the black construction paper to the bottom of the cardboard box to absorb the light and transform it into radiant heat to melt the s'mores.

4. The most delicious part of this process is preparing the s'mores. Students layer the marshmallows on one side of one graham square and chocolate pieces on the other graham square and place them in the solar oven.

5. Obviously, this activity requires good sunlight and decent temperatures. Once they put their treats in the oven, they need to place it where it can get as much sunlight as possible. Students should be

reminded that the reflective lid has the important function of directing the sunlight onto the chocolate and marshmallows.

6. After 15 minutes (the chocolate should be melted by then), the students can remove both the graham crackers from the oven and put them together to make the s'mores.

## Journal Comments by Carol Howe

The students easily understood that if they were to cook s'mores in the solar oven, they would need each of these parts to create solar heat. Armed with these concepts, they built the solar ovens with very little help from the teacher because they understood the purpose of each part.

## Extensions

*Science.* Solar power study can extend to other science explorations, for example, to an inquiry into other inventions that harness the sun's energy. Advanced students may explore what would be involved in a greater cooking challenge than s'mores or how the principles they've learned apply to solar panels. How do solar panels heat a space?

*Social studies.* Solar power also relates to social studies. Students interested in the history of solar invention could learn about the pioneer work of the 1970s in the United States (which later diminished with the loss of investment from the government) and the advances in Germany, Scandinavia, and other countries today. Solar energy as a topic offers many opportunities for them to imagine a different kind of world—solar buildings, homes, appliances, and vehicles.

*Art.* The sun colors the world students live in and affects seasonal changes; the habits of animals; the colors of leaves; and the hue of dawn, daylight, and dusk. Students with artistic interests can explore paintings and photographs that represent the sun in different places throughout the year. They can observe, write responses to, or create art pieces on the different levels of brilliancy and color, as well as the effects on the environment. Locker and Christensen's (2001) *Sky Tree: Seeing Science Through Art* is an excellent source for this, as it blends both science and art in a series of breathtaking paintings and related texts that illustrate such processes as photosynthesis. The power of the sun's position on the "sky tree" is strikingly revealed and can assist students in questioning how other artists understand and represent the sun: Is it a personalized vision? Is it surreal? Does it come from observation? Is it based on anything scientific? What aspect of sunlight does the painting reveal? In this way, students can experiment with their own artistic expressions of the sun.

## Geometry and Art

Adapted from Hammer, Joyce. In Smutny, J. F., & von Fremd, S. F. *Igniting Creativity in Gifted Learners, K–6: Strategies for Every Teacher.* Copyright © 2009, Corwin. pp. 218–219.

---

### What-Where-How Priority List

1. **What** are the greatest needs of my advanced learners right now?

   Visual learning opportunities
   Artistic exploration and interpretation

2. **Where** can I address them at this point?

   Mathematics
   Art

3. **How** do I address their needs in an effective yet reasonable way?

   Have them examine art through mathematics and vice versa
   Arrange for them to work in pairs and share design ideas
   Provide opportunities for them to analyze principles of geometry while interpreting these principles through art designs

---

## Rationale

A major purpose of this activity is to guide elementary-age students to see and appreciate the beauty of mathematics, which is so much more than computation. Too often, mathematics becomes figures, graphs, and numbers on paper. Even when creative teaching occurs in classrooms, it tends to focus more on the cognitive domain than on imagination, intuition, or the arts. It's important to note that in contrast to this tendency, advanced mathematicians and inventors have often discovered in the mathematical universe a thing of great beauty.

James Watson and Francis Crick worked feverishly to solve the structure of the DNA molecule, but guided their work with the unproven intuition that the molecule of life would be beautiful, and so they only considered beautiful molecules like spirals, not ugly, amorphous molecules (Thompson, 2000).

Abstracted from any context, mathematics may seem cold and lifeless to students whose main means of learning is pen-and-paper tasks. But math permeates both the natural and man-made worlds around us. When students encounter the intricate patterns, shapes, and all their variations, they find examples of stunning artistry. In this respect, M. C. Escher's

(Math Academy Online, 2011) work presents a new way of investigating mathematical ideas. His explorations of the geometry of space and unique insight into the spatial relationships between objects yielded startling visual designs. Advanced students immediately sense something unusual in his work and appreciate the whimsy. Inserting a few chameleons inside the polyhedron startles them out of their assumptions and ignites their imaginations.

## Level

Elementary grades

## Application

Mathematics, art

## Description

Teacher Joyce Hammer has found Escher's work highly effective in stimulating spatial reasoning and creativity in advanced students. Here is a summary of her process (Smutny & von Fremd, 2009, pp. 218–219).

Joyce Hammer begins her class on geometry and art by writing the question "Who is M. C. Escher?" in large letters. Posters or prints displaying his work enable students to look closely while the teacher points to specific examples of his techniques. Hammer chooses a few pictures to explain what she finds most unusual and creative about them. As students explore Escher's work (both the prints displayed on the walls and collections of his work available in the classroom), they share what they like, what they find interesting, and any observations they have about his use of geometric shapes and designs. Extended exposure to Escher's creativity can sustain the students' interest and lead to subsequent lessons on tessellations. Here are some prompts to guide student thinking:

- Explore how a figure gradually transforms into another figure. Where does this start to change for you?
- How does the artist use space? By having the figures touch one another (no space between them) what happens for you? What do you like or not like about this?
- What shapes are used? How are they like the shapes you're learning about in geometry? How are they different?

- Can you tell what shapes will not be able to fill the page?
- How do you think tessellations are made?

## Making Tessellations

Hammer has students make designs with pattern blocks, allowing them to experiment with different shapes and sizes. Working alone or in pairs, they keep their designs and the supplies they're using on heavy cardboard so that they can move them easily without disturbing their compositions. As students complete designs, the teacher displays them, and also allows them to take photographs to show their families and friends at home. This is an important step in the process, as it encourages children to explore further how they may create new geometric designs through tessellations.

Another approach recommended is for the teacher or students (with the teacher's guidance) to invent line designs with needle and colorful thread on card stock. The teacher can then tape the designs on the door so that students can see them while entering or leaving the classroom. Students explore the question, How can a straight line look curved? Younger students create their line designs with pencil and straightedge, using simple patterns; more advanced learners create their own. Math catalogs offer line design books with a wide range of illustrated patterns from simple to complex.

Hammer has found that exploring designs made with a compass and straightedge enhances their interest in geometric patterns. Here are her observations:

*I begin by showing various designs arising from one basic shape—the hexagon. Students then gather around and watch as I create the basic shape repeatedly. They then choose which design they want me to make. Slowly, I show how the design evolves from this shape by just darkening and/or drawing some lines, erasing others, and sometimes doing a little shading. As often as needed, I repeat this method of forming the design. Each student has a copy of the basic shape, a sheet showing all the different ones that can be made from it, plenty of plain paper, a pencil, a straightedge, and a good eraser.*

*After students have completed several of the designs from that first basic shape, they learn another one that still stems from a hexagon, but with slight differences. The same teaching method applies in this case and students create new interesting designs. Displaying their designs wherever space permits enhances the desire to do more. The intent of the activity is to enable students to analyze certain designs, determine how to produce identical figures, albeit different sized ones, and complete them successfully, guided by the previous instruction.*

## Extensions

*Art and math.* This process lays the foundation for future tessellation designs, which grow in complexity according to the students' ability and knowledge. It is ideal for advanced learners because they can express mathematical concepts in nontraditional ways. An excellent website for more advanced tessellations is http://www.tessellations.org/. Instructions guide students not only in using the line method but also in slice, gap, multi, circular, and fractal methods as well.

*Art and philosophy.* Advanced students will also enjoy the ways Escher explores the logic of space. In drawing, an artist chooses vanishing points to represent the point at infinity. By designing compositions around unexpected vanishing points, Escher made the orientation of his drawings shift according to how the viewer looked at them. Students can explore the relationship between the line, shape, and proportion of objects in a drawing and the angle of vision; they can investigate this also in their own lives. What role does point of view have on the proportion and shape of things they see? What do Escher's drawings express about the world around him? The nature of things? The way space works? Students can speculate about how they would see the objects, shapes, and space around them if they walked around inside an Escher drawing.

*Biography.* Students who have completed their designs and want to know more about Escher's life can extend their learning through biographical sources (books, websites, etc.). Activities need not culminate in a written biography but could result in a story of an important discovery or event in his life, told through a poster or a collage combining text and Escher-like visual design. Another option would be for students to research a particular interest of Escher's (e.g., the shape of space, tessellations, vanishing points, or perspective), pose a question, and respond through creative fiction, free verse, or artistic design.

## Daily Math Games

Adapted from Freeman, Christopher M. In Smutny, J. F., & von Fremd, S. E. *Igniting Creativity in Gifted Learners, K–6: Strategies for Every Teacher.* Copyright © 2009, Corwin. pp. 205–212.

### What-Where-How Priority List

1. **What** are the greatest needs of my advanced learners right now?

   Inductive thinking
   Fun game activities
   Critical and creative thinking

2. **Where** can I address them at this point?

   Mathematics
   Analytical and creative thinking

3. **How** do I address their needs in an effective yet reasonable way?

   Encourage them to use inductive thinking to discern patterns and rules
   Teach them how to play a competitive game that challenges their problem-solving abilities
   Have them learn collaboratively—by observing and analyzing peer responses

## Rationale

Math games provide advanced students with fun but mentally challenging activities that promote growth in critical and creative thinking. With prompts and support from the teacher, they not only discover patterns that govern the game but create winning strategies by repeated observation and thinking inductively about the process. When placed in suitable groups, students experience noticeable growth from one game to the next. Finally, all students need to learn that mathematics can be fun!

## Level

Middle grades, but adjustable to other levels

## Application

Mathematics, higher-level and divergent thinking

Christopher Freeman, a sixth-grade mathematics teacher and author, shares a few math games that work well for advanced students and require little preparation (Smutny & von Fremd, 2009, pp. 205–212). Though games, these activities teach students mathematical ideas and create an element of fun and excitement in approaching puzzling problems.

## Prime Factorizations

Every day of school, I ask for the prime factorization of the number of the day, for example, Day 24 = 2(to the 3rd) × 3. It's like a game. Students spend years learning to think of numbers in place value, but they also need to think of numbers as products composed of factors. Why? For one thing, when they put fractions into lowest terms, they need to recognize common factors. I also ask students to list the factors of the number of the day. For example, the factors of 36 are 1, 2, 3, 4, 6, 9, 12, 18, and 36. Advanced students enjoy some of the questions I present for them to ponder as we do this activity: Why does 36 have an odd quantity of factors? What kind of numbers all have an odd quantity of factors? And how can you predict how many factors a number will have from its prime factorization?

### Bizz-Buzz Bopp

This is a good game to teach divisibility and factoring skills. Have all the students stand behind their chairs. Clearly define a path to follow, from student to student. Select a random student to begin. The first student says, "One." The next student says, "Two." The students continue in order, each saying the next whole number. But if the number is a multiple of five, the students must say, "Buzz" instead. If the number is a multiple of both three and five, the student must say, "Bizz-buzz" or "Buzz-bizz." Students get five seconds to think. If the student says the wrong thing, she must sit down so that others may count ahead correctly. When there are only two students left, they are joint winners. The goal is for the class to get to 100 with three or more students still in the game. When the students get good at this game, add "bopp" for multiples of four, "bang" for multiples of seven, and "beep" for multiples of 11. Children enjoy the odd conversations: "19," "bopp-buzz," "bizz-bang," "beep," "23." They learn to love prime numbers.

### The 100 Game

Two people play. The first player calls out a whole number from 1 to 10. The players take turns calling out bigger and bigger numbers—never more than 10 higher than the previous number just called out. Whoever says 100 wins. Advanced students quickly realize that if you can say 89, you will win the game because the other player cannot say 100, but whatever number he does say, you can say 100. Let the students play the game several times. Soon, they will find that 78 is also a winning number. Indeed, there is a whole sequence of winning numbers, starting with one. Once a student has found all the winning numbers, have him beat you in whispers. Then, swear him to secrecy! You don't need to use all the winning numbers—unless you are playing someone who knows them all. Otherwise, call out any random numbers you like—but be sure you say 67. Students really like keeping a secret!

### Nim: Variations and Strategies

Mathematicians have studied Nim games for thousands of years. I have used them in my regular sixth-grade classroom (20 minutes every Monday morning for two months).

The basic game has five rules:

1. Two people play.

2. There is one pile.

3. It has 13 objects.

4. At your turn, you may take one or two objects from the pile.

5. Whoever takes the last one loses.

I introduce the game with the innocent-sounding question, "Do you want to go first, or do you want me to go first?" When assisting students in finding the strategy, it is helpful to work backward. Ask, "What can you do if there is one paper clip? Two paper clips? Three? Four?" "Do you see a pattern in these answers?"

When a student has figured out the strategy for this game and beaten me twice, I suggest variations. The first variation is to play with 15 objects, then with 20. The ultimate game is to beat me starting with any number: I say the number; the student must decide whether to go first and take one, go first and take two, or let me go first. I have been known to play this game with students while walking on a field trip. It's fun to see other students' eyes bulge when they hear our conversation: "How many?" "6,489." "I'll take two." "OK, you win. Another game?"

When many students are ready, I teach another variation to the whole group: "At your turn, you may take one, two, or three." Again, we play with 13, then later 15, 20, or any number of objects. Quicker students proceed to further variations; all students enjoy working on the game that is appropriate for them.

The next variations are "Take one, two, three, or four," and then "Take one, two, three, four, or five." Students with some knowledge of algebra may enjoy listing the winning numbers for "Take one, two . . ." When they have done this, I ask them to list the winning numbers for the special case where $k = 10$. They have such delight when the winning numbers of the 100 Game appear!

Another worthwhile variation on Rule 4 is "Take two or three" (but not one). This game introduces the possibility of *tying* positions because if there is only one left, no one is allowed to take it, so no one loses. Some students will even be able to list winning, tying, and losing positions for the general game, "Take $j$ . . . $k$."

So far, we have varied only Rules 3 and 4. To vary other rules, I teach the two-pile game: There are two piles of 6 and 10. At your turn, you may *take as many as you want from one pile or the same number from both piles.* Whoever takes the last one wins. This is actually my favorite game of all. One needs to find and list the winning positions—pairs of numbers that you wish to leave for the other player.

Of course, there is the three-pile game, in which you may *take any number from one pile only,* and whoever takes the last one wins. I often start with three, five, and seven objects in the piles. This is the classic game often referred to as "Nim."

## Calendar Challenge

Adapted from Fisher, Carol. In Smutny, J. F., & von Fremd, S. E. *Igniting Creativity in Gifted Learners, K–6: Strategies for Every Teacher.* Copyright © 2009, Corwin. pp. 224–226.

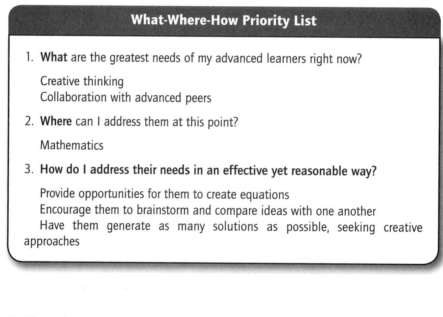

### What-Where-How Priority List

1. **What** are the greatest needs of my advanced learners right now?

   Creative thinking
   Collaboration with advanced peers

2. **Where** can I address them at this point?

   Mathematics

3. **How do I address their needs in an effective yet reasonable way?**

   Provide opportunities for them to create equations
   Encourage them to brainstorm and compare ideas with one another
   Have them generate as many solutions as possible, seeking creative approaches

## Rationale

This strategy is designed to stimulate more creative thinking in mathematics and to enable advanced students to formulate equations. For highly able math learners, it presents unlimited possibilities, as they can use fractions, exponents, and any operations they like as long as they follow the basic framework.

## Level

Intermediate and middle grades and up

## Application

Highly adaptable for an individual, small-group, and whole-class creative process in mathematics, this strategy relates to many math concepts in the curriculum.

Teacher Carol Fisher demonstrates how to make each day's date a mathematical challenge for advanced students (Smutny & von Fremd, 2009, pp. 224–226).

## Description

Calendar challenge is a numerical exercise in creative thinking. The premise is based on an idea from a National Council of Teachers of Mathematics (NCTM) journal from 10 or 12 years ago and is quite simple. Create equations using the number associated with a given month six times. The equation's solutions correspond to the number of days in the month. In September, students use six 9s to make equations with answers 1 through 30. In October, students use six 10s to make equations with answers 1 through 31. The framework allows students to challenge themselves or one another to devise equations that follow a specific format. This can be done as an individual, small-group, or whole-class activity. The equations, as well as the students, grow month by month, as their knowledge, creativity, and algebraic thinking develops. The format can change to give students who typically isolate themselves an opportunity to work in a small-group or whole-group setting. The challenge can be competitive among students, or students can individually challenge themselves in creating equations. There is more than one solution to each part of the task, which builds month by month. No matter how competent a student is in computation, the challenges continue. They can experiment with any operations, negative numbers, fractions, decimals, exponents, factorial, or percentage as long as the given number is the only one employed, and they use it exactly six times for each equation.

In the typical school setting, the teacher introduces calendar challenge during the first week of September. It's best to do a whole-group introduction to ensure a solid understanding of the process. Large chart paper is posted on the walls, usually three sheets, the first numbered from 1 through 10, the second from 11 through 20, and the third from 21 through 30. On the whiteboard (or chalkboard or chart paper), I write six 9s spaced out.

9        9        9        9        9        9

As a group, students find a way to insert mathematic symbols to make the equation = 1. In many situations, providing parentheses to encourage grouping can be helpful. There are multiple solutions in this format.

$$(9 \div 9) \times (9 \div 9) \times (9 \div 9) = 1; (9 + 9) - (9 + 9) + (9 \div 9) = 1;$$

$$(9 - 9) + (9 - 9) + (9 \div 9) = 1$$

Other formats can include using 99, 9.9, $9^9$ (all of which count as two 9s).

$$99 \div 99 \times 9 \div 9 = 1; 9.9 - .9 - 9 + 9 \div 9 = 1; 9^9 \div 9^9 + 9 - 9 = 1$$

Once students demonstrate their understanding of this task, they then have to find equations for two and then three. They can easily create these by making minor operation changes in some of the previous equations.

$(9 \div 9) \times (9 \div 9) \times (9 \div 9) = 1$ can be changed to $(9 \div 9) + (9 \div 9)$ $\times (9 \div 9) = 2$

At this point in the activity, it is helpful to summarize some strategic ideas:

$$(9 - 9) = 0; (9 \div 9) = 1; 99 \div 9 = 11$$

If necessary, review the order of operations. Students then find some of the other equations that correspond to the calendar dates. For any (or all) students who feel frustrated, I guide them to 16, 17, 18, 19, and 20. They can solve all of them by starting with $(9 + 9)$ and the previous strategic combinations.

Knowing the social, emotional, and academic needs of their students should guide teachers in establishing the parameters of the challenge for the first month.

- Set a challenge of finding 10 of the 30 equations during the class.
- Encourage students to find more at home.
- Save the day's work, and then continue another day.
- Ask the class to find as many different solutions for a particular calendar date as they can.

However you decide to implement the first month, keep documentation—the student's individual work, the class chart, how many solutions, and so on. During the first week of October, the teacher resurrects the challenge. Now, it's six 10s for the numbers 1 through 31. Have students refer to their work from September. Does this give them any ideas? This comparison is the springboard to creating algebraic formulas for the different numbers.

$$(9 \div 9) \times (9 \div 9) \times (9 \div 9) = 1; (10 \div 10) \times (10 \div 10) \times (10 \div 10) = 1;$$

$$(a \div a) \times (a \div a) \times (a \div a) = 1$$

Designing this as a yearlong project means that only a few formulas need to be attempted each month. If there is a concept (exponents, decimals, etc.) that correlates with the curriculum, this is an excellent way to keep the excitement going; for example, teachers can challenge students to use an exponent in each equation.

September through December usually progress well, and then in January, many students decide it's impossible to use only ones to make equations for the Numbers 1 through 31. This provides a wonderful opportunity for mathematic discourse among advanced learners. In the spring, calendar challenge usually becomes more competitive, whether for individual, small-group, or whole-class solutions.

In this yearlong activity, both advanced and less advanced math students take away much more than the simple creation of mathematical equations. In terms of the NCTM (2011) standards, teachers enhance representation, connections, communication, reasoning and proof, problem solving, number and operations, and algebra. Each group of students I have taught has given me new insight about the depth of creativity that can be evoked by this mathematic activity.

## Fingerprint Analysis

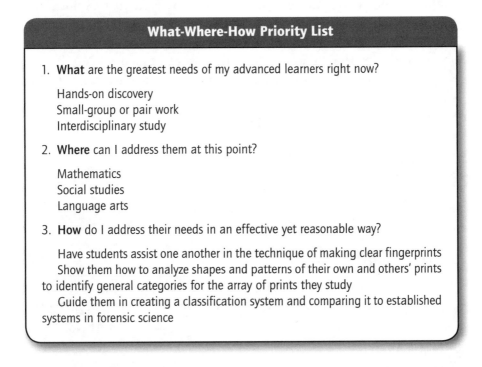

**What-Where-How Priority List**

1. **What** are the greatest needs of my advanced learners right now?

   Hands-on discovery
   Small-group or pair work
   Interdisciplinary study

2. **Where** can I address them at this point?

   Mathematics
   Social studies
   Language arts

3. **How** do I address their needs in an effective yet reasonable way?

   Have students assist one another in the technique of making clear fingerprints
   Show them how to analyze shapes and patterns of their own and others' prints to identify general categories for the array of prints they study
   Guide them in creating a classification system and comparing it to established systems in forensic science

## Rationale

Fingerprint analysis incorporates mathematics and science, and can also extend to other related subjects. It enables advanced students to work together both to assist in making prints as well as in studying patterns and identifying categories.

## Level

Middle grades and up

## Application

Students love posing as forensic scientists, especially as many watch television shows about crime teams taking and analyzing fingerprints. Studying fingerprints enables them to explore not only the evolution of this centuries-old practice to its present-day use in crime detection but also to discover for themselves the principle of variation in every living being. No individual's fingerprints duplicate another's, even in the case of identical twins, and each finger has a different pattern than the others.

## Description

In this study, advanced students create clear prints of their fingers, share them in their groups, take notes on what they observe, and then exchange theirs with those of another group for further exploration. Once all students have shared all the prints (or as many as the teacher has time for), they brainstorm what kind of classification system they could create for the different prints they've examined. This inductive reasoning process exposes students to a wide range of distinguishing shapes and lines.

These are the materials teachers will need:

- Magnifying lens
- Inkpad
- Sheets of paper
- Marking pen

## Making Fingerprints

1. The students make a complete set of their fingerprints. They do this by pressing one finger at a time into the inkpad (avoiding the

mistake of getting their fingers too wet). They work with a partner who holds their hand steady as they press and roll their fingers one at a time onto a clean sheet of white paper. The partner can help them not smudge the prints. Using their marking pens, they then label each print with the name of the finger: thumb, index finger, middle finger, ring finger, pinkie finger.

2. The students look at their fingertips through the magnifying lens and examine the patterns of their skin. The teacher poses questions: Can you describe the shapes and patterns? What are the distinguishing features? What shapes or patterns do you notice the most?

Each small group completes the fingerprinting process so that every student has his labeled prints on a sheet of paper with the student's name clearly written. Next, the teacher has each student make a fingerprint on a separate sheet of paper without any label. When the prints have thoroughly dried, one student turns them face down, shuffles them around, and then chooses one sheet of paper at random. Without calling out the answer, the students take turns studying the print and sharing all the labeled fingerprints on the table. When everyone has had time to examine the evidence, the students share their conclusions with one another, pointing to the patterns and providing a rationale for their answers.

## Classifying Fingerprints

A fingerprint creates an impression on paper of the ridge patterns on the skin. Fingerprints occur because glands in the hands secrete sweat and oil. These liquids leave fingerprint patterns on practically everything they touch. To classify fingerprints, students only need a magnifying lens and several sets of fingerprints. The procedure is as follows:

## Procedure

The teacher exposes students to the different methods for classifying prints. Classification systems break into smaller groups. Forensic scientists divide arches into *plain* arches (rounded) and *tented* arches (pointed). Loops can be *radial* loops, which loop from the right, or *ulnar* loops, which loop from the left. Whorls are also classed into several divisions.

1. Students use the magnifying lens to observe several sets of fingerprints. The teacher poses questions: How are these prints similar? What patterns or shapes? Can you group the prints into categories or types to make it easier to identify them?

2. Students study the patterns while the teacher draws attention to the different forms of the arch and loop. They explore these forms and how they bend to the right or left.

3. Students attempt to match the fingerprints they have collected to one of the common patterns.

## Extension (for advanced students who have completed the previous activities)

The teacher has an empty glass at some distance from where the students are working. The teacher tells one student to go to the glass when no one is watching and pick up the glass. To make good prints, she should rub each finger along her nose or through her hair first, and then press each finger hard on the glass. When the teacher starts the group on a new assignment for fingerprint analysis, the teacher retrieves the glass (using a napkin), announcing that someone drank the water she had in the glass and the group needs to find the culprit. The perpetrator plays along with the group, not letting on that she is the one.

Dusting is one method for locating fingerprints that most students have seen on television. The fingerprints are coated with powder, then lifted off the surface and sent to a lab. The materials needed are as follows:

- Drinking glass
- Cocoa
- Small paintbrush
- Transparent tape
- Sheets of light-colored construction paper

The students sprinkle cocoa on the glass to coat the prints. They then lightly brush the powdered area with a small paintbrush. Once students brush off the loose powder, they can see fingerprints. They lift each print from the glass by placing the sticky side of transparent tape on the dusted print and then carefully lifting the tape from glass. The dusted print should stick to the tape. They then place each piece of tape on a separate sheet of light colored construction paper.

## Other Extensions

Students love learning techniques featured in detective shows or in the murder mystery stories they have read. Advanced students can take the activities learned here and use them as catalysts for other projects in social studies or language arts. Here are some examples:

- Students write a short mystery story where a fingerprint analysis leads to an unlikely suspect.
- They create a series of sketches with descriptions that summarize several major historic discoveries about fingerprints.
- They sketch and paint fingerprint patterns from examples in the class to create an art piece that depicts the concept of uniqueness and variation.
- They compose a free-verse poem on the theme of pattern and design (which could accompany the previous art piece).

These examples represent a variety of creative and practical responses to the needs of advanced students in both science and math. Yet, those who perform at an "average" level also benefit from having new choices that inspire and challenge them. These students may surprise their teachers when they read a short story in record time and then ask if the author has written any others. Likewise, a kinesthetic learner who slumps over his desk during paper-and-pencil tasks suddenly comes alive in a project where he can learn *by doing* (dramatizing a story, constructing a model, or designing an ant farm). Addressing the different needs of advanced students is certainly important. But teachers can also adapt these strategies to embrace a much wider range of learning needs and preferences in their classrooms.

Like those in the previous chapter, the following charts provide examples of adjustments you can make in math and science to meet the needs of advanced students in your classroom. Intended as examples to spur your imagination, they represent different levels of preparation so that you can choose what is most manageable for you. The question always is, How far can I go in planning and supervising a learning option? How do I juggle the needs of a few without neglecting those of the many? The examples here approach this question by showing how it is always possible to do *something*, even if this something is only a slight alteration from the rest of the class—a different use of sources or a change in the thinking process involved. What we hope you do is find—in your repertoire of topics and teaching routines—creative new ways to reignite learning in your classroom.

*Science*

| Learning Needs | High-Preparation Strategies | Low-Preparation Strategies |
|---|---|---|
| New concepts and skills to learn Faster pace Higher-level thinking | **Compacting**<br><br>In a primary grade unit on photosynthesis, advanced students skip direct instruction of concepts and knowledge already mastered to study its relation to the seasons; they draw on observations, reports, books, and interviews of science teachers to create a display that illustrates the process of photosynthesis through the seasons. | **Change Sources**<br><br>Students go to a learning center and select at least two other, more advanced sources (texts, visuals, or websites).<br><br>**Change Thinking Process**<br><br>They select either a higher-level thinking question or a creative process related to photosynthesis (e.g., How does photosynthesis work differently with deciduous versus conifer trees? Students write a free-verse poem on their discovery.) |
| More challenge in class assignments Faster pace New skills and concepts | **Tiered Instruction**<br><br>Tier 1: Students identify and describe the different stages of the rock cycle, and demonstrate how rocks can develop differently.<br><br>Tier 2: They use specimens to apply their knowledge of rock formation to hypothesize how they might have formed; they write and diagram a biography of two different rocks. | **Change Sources**<br><br>Students add to the class unit by doing an Internet search on one stage of the rock cycle that most interests them.<br><br>**Change Thinking Process**<br><br>They demonstrate how color, luster, the Mohs hardness scale, and a streak test help to identify minerals; they compare this process to detective work and explain what mistakes might occur if they eliminated one or more of these steps. |

| Learning Needs | High-Preparation Strategies | Low-Preparation Strategies |
|---|---|---|
| Visual and kinesthetic learning preferences<br><br>Creative media | **Interest Centers**<br><br>Students research and analyze the unique features of birds that make them aerodynamic and how these principles apply to aviation today. They conceptualize and sketch a model airship of their own and explain how weight, lift, thrust, and drag operate in their design. | **Choices in Sources and Processes**<br><br>Students explore books related to flight, including stories about flying from different cultures—such as Icarus in ancient Greece or the flying slaves, escaping the plantations in America. They analyze what message they think these stories meant to convey to the people who heard them. |
| Immersion study<br><br>In-depth inquiry<br><br>Interdisciplinary study | **Independent Study**<br><br>Students conduct a two-week study of another planet in the solar system and examine its livability—analyzing the elements that would present particular problems for organic life. They explore the latest research on the planet and compare what the world knows now to earlier ideas about the solar system. | **Simpler Explorations**<br><br>In a life science class, students keep a nature journal with daily entries on animal visitors to the yard (or park) and particularly on behaviors. They explore the following question after regular and repeated observations: What do you think a particular animal behavior is about and how did you come to this conclusion? |

*Mathematics*

| Learning Needs | High-Preparation Strategies | Low-Preparation Strategies |
|---|---|---|
| Fast readers<br>Higher-level thinkers<br>Skilled writers | **Tiered Instruction**<br><br>Tier 1: Students use visual thinking to create a design, practice measurement skills, | **Change Sources**<br><br>Students tackle number patterns, visualizing relationships, and analyzing |

*(Continued)*

(Continued)

| Learning Needs | High-Preparation Strategies | Low-Preparation Strategies |
|---|---|---|
| | and calculate lengths to make three-dimensional objects.<br><br>Tier 2: They apply their knowledge of geometric shapes and measurement skills to research kite design and build tetrahedron kites. | the operations between seemingly random numbers.<br><br>**Change Thinking Process**<br><br>They create a number pattern of their own, which they then exchange with other advanced students to develop flexible thinking and problem solving. |
| Strong Interests: Culture Map-making Current events<br><br>Connections to real-world issues and problems | **Interest Centers**<br><br>Students explore features on a globe, read and interpret a scale, compute distances using a scale factor, and find the perimeter and area of landmasses. They sharpen world geography skills as they review map terminology, create a map, and explore and discuss a Mercator projection. | **Extension Activities**<br><br>Students research the process by which Gerardus Mercator created his projection of the Earth. They analyze the distortions in landmass that this projection creates the farther one gets from the equator. |
| Visual and kinesthetic learning preferences Creative media | **Arts Integration**<br><br>Students study how artists incorporate math in creating their visual works. They examine "cubism" in Picasso's paintings and explore ways to incorporate geometric solids into their art. Following this exploration, they create an art piece that expresses some aspect of cubism. | **Choices in Sources and Processes**<br><br>Based on their knowledge of geometric shapes, students measure, compare, and draw different kinds of simple and compound leaves in a journal of leaves. They draw geometric shapes within natural ones—triangles at the ends of leaves, rectangles in branches, a circle within an acorn)—and explain how this helps identify species in nature. |

| Learning Needs | High-Preparation Strategies | Low-Preparation Strategies |
|---|---|---|
| Immersion study In-depth inquiry Interdisciplinary study | **Independent Study**<br><br>The students track a baseball team for one month and predict how the team will perform based on players' scoring patterns and abilities. They analyze data and explore the team's history, fan culture, and ball park stories to create a baseball poster for the class. | **Simpler Explorations**<br><br>Students explore the relationship between architecture and math. They apply the principles of building and engineering by first drafting a plan and then measuring, cutting, drilling, and joining to create small models of structures (e.g., domes, igloos, bridges, and dams). |

## PARTING THOUGHTS FOR YOUR JOURNEY

*Allow for accelerated learning.* Students who are advanced in science and math crave more challenging content at a faster pace than they typically receive in school. Teachers often wonder what would happen if these learners completed the year's planned curriculum early. Try not to let this concern prevent you from exploring all options for students who clearly need accelerated instruction. First, consider what you can do. What adjustments can you make for these students in alternative assignments, independent studies, paired instruction, and so forth? Next, involve others—fellow teachers, curriculum coordinators, administrators, and parents. Clarify what you can and cannot do, given the demands on your time, and request assistance. We have seen new opportunities for student learning emerge from this openness. They range from parents and community members assisting in the classroom (as mentors), to higher-grade math or science teachers including advanced students from a lower grade, to teachers in a school creating math and science clubs for gifted learners.

*Include creative exploration and expression.* As shown in the examples, advanced students are always looking for new ways to approach these subjects, which include artistic expressions of mathematic or scientific principles. Once students acquire skill and knowledge in an area, they can apply what they know in more creative ways. Whenever possible, try to design mathematic or scientific processes that allow more choices in how students use their knowledge and communicate their discoveries (e.g., handwritten explanations, designs, computer graphics, drawings, or dramatizations). Use open questioning to inspire as many new approaches to problems as they can find. Help them shift from a find-the-solution mind-set to a more creative challenge: How many possible solutions might there be to this problem, and how many can you find?

*Focus on mysteries.* Advanced students cannot help becoming curious about an unexplained phenomenon. As mentioned earlier in the case of the giant squid in northern California, a scientific or mathematic curiosity of the week—displayed enticingly for all to see—can transform a unit into a puzzler that students want to mull over and solve. Walking into the classroom on any day, advanced students need to experience some degree of wonderment—to realize that curious and little-known facts could appear in any subject and that they could open a new world to them. It's important to preserve the magical quality of your mysteries. How does the New Caledonian Crow make tools? What is unusual about "hyperbolic space" as seen in M. C. Escher's representations, and what would it be like to walk in that space? What creatures have *bioluminescence,* and how does it work? Encourage students to bring in their puzzlers and mystery questions for you to unveil at the beginning of the week. This routine helps students relate to science and math as real worlds inhabited by live beings, strange phenomena, and countless systems yet to be discovered.

# Keeping Yourself Inspired

It is the supreme art of the teacher to awaken joy in creative expression and knowledge.

—Albert Einstein

I am not a teacher but an awakener.

—Robert Frost

The great teacher is not the man who supplies the most facts, but the one in whose presence we become different people.

—Ralph Waldo Emerson

**M**any teachers feel like satellites spiraling around a great ball of energy. It's easy to feel taxed by the responsibilities of teaching when you're trying to respond to the needs of so many different students at once. Being aware of your need for replenishment and inspiration can be difficult.

Often, teachers think they have to plan for every step in a process, to anticipate needs and create variations of an assignment, "just in case." This is all part of good teaching, but one can also overplan to such a degree that students don't have to do much more than show up. Now and then, we should ask ourselves, How much is too much? Am I micro-managing every moment? Am I underestimating the extent to which my students can assume responsibilities? Am I making room for normal human error? Is the pressure on my school to turn out high-achieving students forcing me to become more concerned about successful outcomes for every activity? Consider the following chart to gauge where you feel you are.

---

### Do you need more balance?

How do you know when you need a breather, when you're becoming so concerned about meeting district demands that it affects your teaching?

- Do you spend more time focusing on how to keep your teaching in line with district requirements than on acting on your instincts as a teacher?
- Do you easily feel concerned if you make an error or miscalculate the time it took to complete a unit?
- Do you see your students as depending entirely on you for their growth and progress as learners?
- Do you assume that a visiting parent or principal is going to judge you?
- Do you get upset if your students don't achieve the grades or test scores you feel they should, given the time and effort you put into their preparation?
- If your students struggle, do you feel it's your fault?
- Do you have downtime in the classroom? Time for fun, light-heartedness, and joy?

---

These are just some of the questions to consider. Balance is what you need most in your relationships with your students, and this comes through stepping back, freeing yourself from the external pressures enough so that you can breathe, think, and plan. Realize that your primary responsibility is to support your students' abilities to learn and grow in different ways. You can only provide the opportunity and environment to make learning happen; you cannot always determine outcomes. For many teachers, the sense of responsibility for everything that happens and everything that *should* happen makes every expectation hang on their necks like an albatross. It's important to step back now and then and realize how unrealistic this is. We know that in life, we don't control circumstances or people as much as we might like; all we can truly control are *our choices and responses*—our attitudes; our decisions about how to approach the demands on our time; our behavior toward our students, colleagues, and administrators; and our thoughts and actions when difficulties rise. Worrying about the standards, learning benchmarks, and other goals can be debilitating, especially as education is not a factory system where one can determine product output ahead of time.

At the center of education are young human beings, each with his or her own way of thinking and learning, each having a unique history, community, and culture. There is a science to teaching, but also an art, as you have discovered many times. For example, if your students come alive in a mural project, you may decide to capitalize on this, building visual art into other units to extend learning. Or you may have an advanced student who barely exerts herself in math but becomes more enthused as you begin to create assignments that are more challenging for her. Or you teach a unit on immigration that takes off when students begin writing free-verse poems to tell their family stories. These are all part of the adventure—the small blessings that make your life in the classroom exciting and inspiring.

## GIVE YOURSELF SOME FRESH AIR

Part of being a good advocate for your students, including your most advanced learners, is keeping yourself going—not letting criticism deflate you, not letting closed doors defeat you, and, perhaps most important, not neglecting to feed your inner life. You need support and people to talk to. You need a sense of perspective and time away—even if only an hour or a day.

Whatever your circumstances, give yourself some fresh air. Time and space for you to do something *you* really care about are essential. No matter how difficult it may seem to manage, try to carve out some little niche in the day or week to do what you love. Try not to let yourself become so depleted by the demands of your teaching that you feel empty and drained. If we think metaphorically for a moment and regard teachers as oil lamps, the light they shed is what reaches their students through the lessons they teach, as well as their kindness and support for each one's growth; the oil is what feeds *them*. Sometimes, when the demands and responsibilities increase, teachers keep going, almost on automatic, forgetting to replenish their oil. From time to time, it's helpful to remember: Give your light, but not your oil. The oil is yours!

While we are busy teaching, it's also easy to forget that our students are watching *us* to see how they should feel about their learning, how they should respond to challenges, how they should act when things don't go well, and how they should regard their interests and needs. E. Paul Torrance, the great pioneer in creativity research, had a marvelous piece of advice in an article he wrote for *Creative Child and Adult Quarterly.* You may find, as we do, that it applies just as well to adults as to students. It's a short piece called "The Importance of Falling in Love With 'Something'" (1983):

1. Don't be afraid to fall in love with something and pursue it with intensity and depth.

2. Know, understand, take pride in, practice, develop, use, exploit, and enjoy your greatest strengths.

3. Learn to free yourself from the expectations of others and to walk away from the games that others try to impose upon you. Free yourself to "play your own game" in such a way as to make good use of your gifts.

4. Don't waste a lot of expensive energy trying to do things for which you have little ability or love. Do what you can do well and what you love, giving freely of the infinity of your greatest strengths and most intense loves.

For young minds, nothing is more catching than a teacher's enthusiasm for some activity or subject he loves. More than content and skills, students learn lessons about growth and living by watching their teacher—lessons that, years later, may still be indelibly imprinted on their minds. They see in their impassioned teacher a living example of what it means to love learning and to pursue one's goals with energy and determination. Consider ways that you can share more of your interests with them. How might you involve them in projects related to a volunteer organization you've joined? An art practice you've been involved in for years? A lifelong passion for a craft, a science, or a literary genre?

Think about yourself as a person in your own right. What are your needs? What would you like to do if you had the time? How can you create time and space to do this? Can you find a little time for yourself each day? Every other day? Twice a week?

Start however you can, big or small. But make the start. As you replenish yourself, you'll be renewing your energy and zest for all the young people who trek into your room day after day, looking for something to inspire them. And if you're like many teachers we know, you find in the students themselves an endless supply of ideas and questions to explore.

Recently, we asked a couple of teachers we know how they recharge themselves. These were their responses.

"I have to take time for myself. I go to the theater, read my books, and visit museums. I take my dog on long walks in the forest preserve to get away from things, but because that is good thinking time, I often come up with solutions. I try to visit museums as often as I can. I keep my eyes open, always looking for new questions that I want to answer myself. I listen to my students' questions because they have great ones."

"I never take things for granted. I wonder and question things myself. I like being questioned. Why and why not aren't just for two-year-olds; they are inquiries worthy of everyone's consideration—especially, the why nots."

## SHARE YOUR WISDOM AND PASSION

We do a great service to advanced students when we help them find a sense of purpose—by our personal example and by guiding them and giving them room to grow. Many talented young people get good grades, but this rarely satisfies them. They hunger for something more fulfilling—a sense of connection to others, an inner resilience in holding onto their dreams and aspirations.

There is a story about a man who came upon hundreds of small starfish washed up on the shore. As he began throwing them back into the ocean, another man approached and asked what he was doing. The first man replied that the starfish had been washed up out of the sea and needed to return to the water. Would the second man help? The other man wondered what the point of all this would be when he wouldn't be able to get them all back. He asked what difference it would make. The first man then picked up a starfish, tossed it into the sea, and replied, "It makes a difference to this one" (Herring, n.d.).

As teachers, we play a key role in helping students discover their niche in the world and, in essence, returning them to their natural element—to the passion and the work that gives them joy. This is what we work for in advocating for advanced students. The author bell hooks pays tribute to this kind of advocacy when she tells of the extraordinary women in her family who helped her to stand on her own feet. Speaking of the influence her grandmother's quiltmaking had on her, she writes the following:

> Fascinated by the work of her hands, I wanted to know more, and she was eager to teach and instruct, to show me how one comes to know beauty and give oneself over to it. To her, quiltmaking was a spiritual process where one learned surrender. . . . This was

the way she had learned to approach quiltmaking from her mother. To her it was an art of stillness and concentration, a work which renewed the spirit. (hooks, 1990, p. 116)

Hooks goes on to explain how she found inspiration for her work from the quilt her grandmother gave her:

Since my creative work is writing, I proudly point to ink stains on this quilt which mark my struggle to emerge as a disciplined writer. . . . This quilt (which I intend to hold onto for the rest of my life) reminds me of who I am and where I have come from. (hooks, 1990, pp. 121–122)

The quilt performed a special service for bell hooks. It affirmed, in a tangible way, her heritage, a heritage she could remember and draw on whenever she needed to. Woven into the fabric of the quilt was also the strength, sureness, and deep spirituality of her grandmother, who gave bell hooks the special support she needed to embrace her gifts.

It's our fervent desire that this book fulfill a similar purpose for you and, through you, for your students. We've tried to show how you can make and share your quilts, invested with passion, commitment, affirmation, and the courage to create. Work steadily but patiently on your quilt. Take fulfillment in both its beauty and its flaws. Involve your students in the process so they can apply themselves to expanding the quilt and creating designs of their own making.

You can give your students no greater gift.

# Resources

A comprehensive list of resources for advanced students could comprise a volume in and of itself. What follows is a list of resources known specifically by us or by the many teachers with whom we consulted. It is a rich sampling of treasures yet to be discovered! We hope it inspires you to explore and investigate your own promising leads.

## GENERAL

### Teacher Vision

http://www.teachervision.fen.com/

This website presents a wide range of teaching strategies in all subject areas, incorporating curriculum standards at every step. Through a reasonably priced subscription, teachers can gain access to 20,000 pages of classroom-ready lesson plans, printables, clip art, and other resources. Visitors can test the site's usefulness through a seven-day free trial that includes two free printable books, *Teacher Timesavers, Volumes 1 and 2.*

### Lesson Planet

http://www.lessonplanet.com

The site offers more than 150,000 lesson plans, all reviewed and rated by credentialed K–12 teachers. It provides an easy search by grade level and subject and connects to state standards. There is a small subscription to join.

### Education World

http://www.educationworld.com

This exceptional resource includes a search engine for educational websites, lesson plans, technology, articles, daily features, and columns. A key goal of the site is to simplify the process of finding and integrating the rich sources of the Internet into the classroom.

## Teachers Net

http://teachers.net/

This is an exceptional site of more than 3,000 free lesson plans in all subjects, at all grade levels, as well as many useful teaching tools and project ideas developed *by* teachers *for* teachers. The site offers active teacher discussion boards and chat rooms that connect educators across the nation, and it provides up-to-date information on thousands of teaching jobs and career resources.

## United Streaming

http://streaming.discoveryeducation.com

A browser-based Internet content delivery system developed by Discovery Education, this link offers approximately 5,000 standards-based educational videos (and 40,000 chaptered clips of videos) as well as teacher's guides, blackline masters, student activities, clip art, quizzes, and other teacher tools. It also provides professional development resources with a video library of best practices, live web seminars, technological demonstrations, and tips on using educational software.

## Amazing Kids!

http://www.amazing-kids.org/home

Amazing Kids! is an online magazine by and for kids. Based in California with volunteers around the globe, it seeks to nurture the unique talents of kids by providing access to mentors and inspiring them to pursue excellence in all endeavors. Amazing Kids! offers quality educational programs, including the Amazing Kids! online magazine where young authors can publish their work and read the submissions of others their age.

## MENTOR: The National Mentoring Partnership

http://www.mentoring.org

For more than 20 years, MENTOR has taken a leading role in advocating and supporting youth mentoring in the United States. This is an excellent resource for mentors and mentoring initiatives across the United States. Teachers and other adults can find guidance and resources to assist them in meeting the educational needs of advanced students through mentorship. The site has step-by-step instructions on developing a mentoring program, and also lists a variety of organizations that connect mentors with young people.

## Self-Efficacy Intervention

http://www.gifted.uconn.edu/siegle/SelfEfficacy/section0.html

This site is an extraordinary asset to any teacher seeking guidance on how to increase students' confidence in their ability to achieve and perform well in school. Research demonstrates a high correlation between a student's self-efficacy and high achievement. Developed by Dr. Del Siegle (Neag Center for Gifted Education and Talent Development, University of Connecticut), the site presents clear directions on strategies that most effectively enhance self-efficacy in the classroom.

## Hoagies' Gifted Education Page

www.hoagiesgifted.org

The award-winning Hoagies' website offers a staggering range of resources for educators and parents of gifted youth. With more than 1,000 pages of information on gifted children and adults, teachers cannot miss any facet of the life and learning of advanced students. All the resources listed on Hoagies' pages are recommended by parents, teachers, psychologists, and/or gifted students themselves.

## LANGUAGE ARTS AND SOCIAL STUDIES

### Literature Circles Resource Center

http://www.litcircles.org

Designed by Dr. Katherine Schlick Noe, the Literature Circles Resource Center makes the most current research and resources on literature circles available to elementary and middle school teachers. This interactive site includes a wide range of guidelines, book lists, and resources that change periodically. Visitors to the site can download forms and informational sheets to adapt to the needs of their students.

## Teacher Resources

http://www.lauracandler.com/strategies/litcirclemodels.php

Created by a middle school teacher with 30 years in the classroom, Teacher Resources includes excellent resources and strategies for anyone who wants to implement literature circles but needs guidance on the best resources and strategies for getting started. From years of experimenting with different models, she offers advice on how teachers can effectively launch a literature circle program tailored to the needs of their students. The site also provides printable materials to assist the process.

## Academy of Achievement

http://www.achievement.org

Among the many resources offered by this extraordinary website are Achievement TV and Achieve Net Curriculum. Achievement TV is a library of outstanding video programs on the greatest pioneers and contributors to the arts, business, public service, science, exploration, and sports. It includes supporting materials such as teacher's guides and student handouts. Achieve Net Curriculum has designed excellent materials for Grades 4 through 12 and post 12th grade.

## English Companion

http://englishcompanion.ning.com

A two-year winner of the Edublog Award for Best Educational Use of Social Networking, English Companion Ning pools together a rich variety of conversations, groups, and blog postings from English and language arts teachers from all over the world. Visitors can find useful ideas on every conceivable facet of teaching English as the site has thousands of pages of award-winning K–12 materials and classroom-tested strategies.

## ReadWriteThink

http://www.readwritethink.org/

This is another exceptional website for educators, parents, and others who seek the highest-quality resources and strategies for instruction in reading and the language arts. An added bonus is the focus on the best materials available *for free*. All lesson plans are aligned not only to the International Reading Association/National Council of Teachers of English (IRA/NCTE) Standards for the English Language Arts but to those of individual states as well.

## iEARN: International Education and Resource Network

http://www.iearn.org/

A nonprofit organization, iEARN includes more than 30,000 schools and youth organizations in more than 130 countries. This site enables teachers and young people to engage in collaborative project work using the Internet and other new communications technologies. It offers more than 150 projects for teachers to adapt to their curriculum and student needs.

## DocsTeach: The National Archives Experience

http://docsteach.org/

The National Archives has created a website to help educators teach with primary source documents. The site enables teachers to explore thousands of documents in a variety of media from the National Archives holdings. It also provides online tools to help teachers combine these materials and create engaging history lessons that students can access over the Internet. Docs Teach activities are categorized according to the National History Standards.

## Making Books With Children

www.makingbooks.com

A book artist, Susan Kapuscinski Gaylord has made books with thousands of children of all ages. Her website demonstrates how the creative art of book making integrates with subject areas and targets fundamental learning goals. A teacher herself for 20 years, Gaylord discovered that students cannot wait to begin writing in books they have fashioned with their own hands. A video on the site demonstrates her process.

## Books to Explore

Ada, A. F. (2003). *A magical encounter: Latino children's literature in the classroom.* Boston, MA: Allyn & Bacon.

Cox, P. (2002). *Tell me the continents*. Marion, IL: Pieces of Learning.

Finney, S. (2001). *Keep the rest of the class reading . . . while you teach small groups: 60 high-interest reproducible activities—perfect for learning centers—that build comprehension, vocabulary, and writing skills*. New York, NY: Scholastic.

Hill, B. C., Schlick Noe, K. L., & King, J. A. (2003). *Literature circles in middle school: One teacher's journey*. Norwood, MA: Christopher-Gordon.

Jones, J. J. (1998). *Chalk stories of extraordinary African-Americans*. Marion, IL: Pieces of Learning.

Myers, R. E. (2002). *Wordplay: Language lessons for creative learners*. Marion, IL Pieces of Learning.

National Women's History Project. (1986). *101 wonderful ways to celebrate women's history*. Windsor, CA: National Women's History Project.

Polette, N. (1989). *The best ever writing models from children's literature*. O'Fallon, MO: Book Lures.

Schlick Noe, K. L., & Johnson, N. J. (1999). *Getting started with literature circles*. Norwood, MA; Christopher-Gordon.

## SCIENCE AND MATHEMATICS

### International Telementor Program

http://www.telementor.org

This program is a recognized leader in telementoring. Students gain access to the real world of math, science, and technology fields. The program teams students in 5th through 12th grade with professional adults who become e-mail pen pals and electronic coaches who assist with projects and provide focus and inspiration for their interests.

### The Futures Channel

http://www.thefutureschannel.com

The Futures Channel uses new media technologies to connect students with scientists, engineers, and explorers—thus providing real-life contexts for the concepts they're learning. It works with schools, publishers, science centers, public television stations, web sources, and more to design high-quality digital content to enhance student learning in the classroom.

### goENC

http://www.goenc.com/

The goENC site offers math and science teachers in kindergarten through 12th grade more than 27,000 print and multimedia sources and materials for immediate application to the classroom. One of the few websites ranked highly in both the math and science fields, it offers exceptional web-based resources for a nominal yearly subscription.

## General Explorations in Math and Science (GEMS)

http://lhsgems.org/sequences.html

A highly innovative source for instruction in science and mathematics, GEMS presents a wide range of clearly organized, easy-to-use teacher's guides that address specific areas of knowledge and skill in an engaging way. Aligned with state standards, these science and math guides do not require teachers to have specialized knowledge in these subjects, and all can be used to develop complete units.

## Seeds of Science/Roots of Reading

http://www.scienceandliteracy.org/

This website offers second- through fifth-grade teachers a highly effective approach for integrating science and literacy instruction. Students explore science concepts in depth while increasing their skills in reading, writing, and communication—as scientists do. The units save time by integrating the two subjects and include high-quality student books, materials (for hands-on activities), assessments, and teacher's guides.

## The Botball Educational Robotics Program

http://www.botball.org

This innovative program engages middle and high school students in a team-oriented robotics competition based on national science education standards. By designing, building, programming, and documenting robots, students use science, engineering, technology, math, and writing skills in hands-on projects that extend their learning.

## learningscience.org

http://www.learningscience.org/

This wonderful site is a forum for sharing the newer learning tools of science education that help make science learning the exciting endeavor that it is. Examples to be found include real-time data collection, simulations, inquiry-based lessons, interactive web lessons, remote instrumentation, microworlds, imaging, and more. Drawing on the

National Science Education Standards as a framework, the site features some of the best web sources for science concepts.

## Mad Sci Network

http://www.madsci.org/

Begun as a student-run organization for K–12 students in St. Louis, MadSci Network soon became a popular interactive science-teaching tool for students around the world—maintained by volunteer scientists and engineers. It fields questions in 26 different subjects, covering topics in astronomy, biology, chemistry, computer science, earth sciences, engineering, and physics. No science teacher should be without it! Its free ask-an-expert service and associated web-based resources are invaluable.

## National Library of Virtual Manipulatives

http://nlvm.usu.edu

This site offers a collection of interactive, computer-based math manipulatives for all ages, including young children. A National Science Foundation–supported project, the Library seeks to stimulate a high level of engagement in all things mathematic through its interactive learning tools. Activities align with the National Council of Teachers of Mathematics Standards.

## Math Solutions

http://www.mathsolutions.com/

Recognized leader in mathematics instruction, Marilyn Burns established Math Solutions to empower school districts across the country. The website links visitors to some of the best books in mathematics as well as other tips and resources that enhance effective math instruction in the classroom. Based on Burns's extensive experience and on the most current research on how students learn math, the site provides a powerful forum for teachers to design winning strategies of their own.

## Books to Explore

### Christopher Freeman Books

A math teacher in the upper grades at the University of Chicago Laboratory School, Christopher Freeman has authored a number of innovative (and fun) books that integrate inductive thinking into math lessons of all kinds. Students think inductively when they find winning strategies for math games, formulate hypotheses about the structure of many-pointed stars, or discover which polygons fit together to form polyhedra—and why. Favorites published through Prufrock Press include *NIM: Serious Math With a Simple Game* (2005), *Drawing Stars and Building Polyhedra* (2005), and *Compass Constructions: Activities for Using a Compass and Straightedge* (2010).

### David Schwartz Books

http://davidschwartz.com/

One of the most whimsical writers of math and science books for students, David Schwartz has designed a website as light-hearted and informative as his books. The site features not only his latest books and some excellent resources but he has added a blog on all his recent adventures and ponderings. With almost 50 books, Schwartz has mastered the art of engaging students in math, science, literature, and the odd quirks of everyday life. His site expresses the magic of *How Much Is a Million? G is for Googol, Q is for Quark, If You Hopped Like a Frog, If Dogs Were Dinosaurs*—all favorites among curious students of all ages.

### Ed Zaccarro Math Books

Ed Zaccarro's math books are an extraordinarily rich supplement to any mathematics curriculum; for many teachers, though, his books have become the texts of choice. In addition to the imaginative way he links math concepts with the real world, Zaccarro presents math content at different achievement levels and in ways that stimulate genuine interest and curiosity. Favorites include *Becoming a Problem-Solving Genius* (2006), *Challenge Math* (2005), *Real World Algebra* (2001), *25 Real Life Math Investigations That Will Astound Teachers and Students* (2007), and *Ten Things All Future Mathematicians and Scientists Must Know (But Are Rarely Taught)* (2003).

Assouline, S. (2005). *Developing math talent: A guide for educating gifted and advanced learners in math.* Waco, TX: Prufrock Press.

Bass, J. E., Contant, T. L., & Carin, A. A. (2008). *Teaching science as inquiry* (11th ed.). Upper Saddle River, NJ: Merrill.

Burns, M. (2007). *About teaching mathematics: A K–8 resource* (3rd ed.). Sausalito, CA: Math Solutions.

Campbell, B., & Fulton, L. (2003). *Science notebooks: Writing about inquiry.* Portsmouth, NH: Heinemann.

Hammerman, E., & Musial, D. (2008). *Integrating science with mathematics & literacy: New visions for learning and assessment.* Thousand Oaks, CA: Corwin.

Keeley, P. (2005). *Science curriculum topic study: Bridging the gap between standards and practice.* Thousand Oaks, CA: Corwin.

See also P. Keeley's excellent series: *Uncovering Student Ideas in Science: 25 Formative Assessment Probes* (NSTA Press). Volumes 1–4. Arlington, VA: National Science Teachers Association Press.

Sheffield, L. J. (2003). *Extending the challenge in mathematics: Developing mathematical promise in K–8 students.* Thousand Oaks, CA: Corwin.

# ARTS

## ChildDrama.com

www.childdrama.com/mainframe.html

This site is a lively entrée into using drama in the classroom and also in applying it to all subject areas. Designed by playwright and drama teacher Matt Buchanan, the website provides excellent resources for classroom teachers. Anyone seeking plays for young thespians or lesson plans that incorporate the dramatic arts will find useful resources here—practical and professional guidance in adapting theater to the classroom, proven monologues, materials, books, and websites.

## Mike Venezia

http://www.mikevenezia.com/

Mike Venezia's books are an artistically rich resource for classroom applications of all kinds. Teachers can explore creative extensions through his popular *Getting to Know* series (*Getting to Know the World's Greatest Artists, Getting to Know the World's Greatest Composers, Getting to Know the U.S. Presidents, Getting to Know the World's Greatest Inventors and Scientists*). The books are ideal for students of all ages, as they are beautifully rendered, short enough to be woven into any unit, and hilarious and fun to explore by anyone at any age.

## Chris Van Allsburg

http://www.chrisvanallsburg.com/

Winner of the Caldecott Medal for *Jumanji* (1982) and *The Polar Express* (1985), which he both wrote and illustrated, Chris Van Allsburg has created a whimsical site for enticing visitors into the world of fictional character Harris Burdick. Teachers and students enter *The Mysteries of*

*Harris Burdick* and are immediately captivated. With highly evocative images and captions, the mysteries beckon the imagination. Students cannot resist weaving their tales of adventure and suspense in response to such powerful writing catalysts.

## M. C. Escher

http://www.mcescher.com

Teachers have used M. C. Escher's work for its creative links to mathematics. As an introduction, this website offers biographical information, news, a bibliography (if visitors wish to seek other sources), links, and a virtual ride through some of his works. The galleries provide rare views of the extraordinary range of his creative output.

## Tessellations.org

http://www.tessellations.org/

Inspired by M. C. Escher, this website is one of the best guides for information on the history and development of his remarkable tessellations, as well as clear directions on how to design and produce them. The workshops on *doing* them are extensive and offer a wide range of options for teachers. Galleries of work by school students demonstrate the creative possibilities.

## The Arts in Every Classroom

www.learner.org/libraries/artsineveryclassroom/abtusing.html

This site introduces K–5 teachers to a collection of video programs—each offering a variety of practical strategies and examples that viewers can apply to their classrooms. Video footage, shot in schools around the country, shows teachers using the arts in a variety of successful ways. A print guide and companion website serve as a professional development resource for anyone interested in integrating the arts into the curriculum.

## Art in Action

http://www.artinaction.org/

This website is dedicated to Art in Action, a program that assists teachers in bringing visual arts education to the classroom. Through an innovative, hands-on curriculum that focuses on art history, art appreciation, and art techniques, the program enhances academic and creative growth in a variety of ways. The website is a critical adjunct to the program, providing excellent resources (both web-based and print) for integrating a standards-based visual art program that can make a difference in how students learn.

## Arts Education Partnership

http://www.aep-arts.org/

The Arts Education Partnership is indispensable for any teacher who wants the arts to thrive in American schools. It provides the most current information on arts education policies and activities as they are developing at the national, state, and local levels. The site also functions as a clearinghouse for a number of seminal studies on the arts as applied to student learning and social/emotional development.

## Books to Explore

Bany-Winters, L. (1997). *Onstage: Theatre games and activities for kids.* Chicago, IL: Chicago Review Press.

Efland, A. (2002). *Art and cognition: Integrating the visual arts in the curriculum.* New York, NY: Teachers College Press.

Heinig, R. B. (1987). *Creative drama resource book: Kindergarten through grade 3.* Englewood Cliffs, NJ: Prentice Hall.

Heinig, R. B. (1987). *Creative drama resource book: Grades 4–6.* Englewood Cliffs, NJ: Prentice-Hall.

Khatena, J., & Khatena, N. (1999). *Developing creative talent in art: A guide for parents and teachers.* Stamford, CT: Ablex.

Locker, T., & Christensen, C. (2001). *Sky tree: Seeing science through art.* New York, NY: HarperCollins.

Rich, B. (Ed.). (2005). *Partnering arts education: A working model from ArtsConnection.* New York, NY: Dana Press.

Spolin, V. (1986). *Theater games for the classroom: A teacher's handbook.* Evanston, IL: Northwestern University Press.

St. James, R., & Christensen, J. (1996). *A journey of the imagination: The art of James Christensen: As told by Renwick St. James.* Seymour, CT: The Greenwich Workshop Press.

## TECHNOLOGY

## From Now On

http://fno.org/

From Now On is an educational technology journal that provides useful guidance for teachers trying to navigate the maze of applications and resources for their classrooms. There is a need for articles such as those shared here, as teachers rarely have the time or opportunity to carefully consider the long-term consequences of their technology choices in the classroom. From Now On provides clear-headed thinking about the benefits of the resources available as well as the common pitfalls that arise from excessive or inappropriate use.

## Electronic Portfolios

http://electronicportfolios.org/

Developed by Dr. Helen Barrett, a pioneer in the use of technology for designing student portfolios, this site introduces visitors to the possibilities of using student portfolios in an electronic format. Teachers will find practical assistance and many links for exploring this option for their students.

## 4Teachers

http://www.4teachers.org/

This is an exceptional resource that supports the integration of innovative technologies into the classroom. Among the site's offerings are ready-to-apply web lessons, quizzes, rubrics, classroom calendars, and other tools to support student learning. It also provides professional development opportunities for teachers.

## Edutopia

http://www.edutopia.org/

Designed by the George Lucas Educational Foundation, this website enables students to experience interactive learning environments and to use diverse digital media sources. Through these technologies and the use of best practices, teachers can design strategies that emphasize project-based learning, innovation, and skill development for the 21st century. Edutopia's offering is extensive—in the topics covered, the blogs, the reports from the field, and in the video collection that teachers can use to extend learning in their classrooms.

## Internet 4 Classrooms (i4c)

http://www.internet4classrooms.com/

This is a valuable online resource for teachers who feel the need for support and guidance in using the Internet effectively. It offers a free web portal for teachers, parents, and students who need innovative, high-quality Internet resources without subscription or other charges. Teachers and students can easily enhance classroom instruction, curriculum content, and project ideas. Online technology tutorials are also available.

### The Teacher Tap

http://eduscapes.com/tap/

This site focuses on the use of technology in all facets of teaching and learning. A free resource for both educators and librarians, it provides easy access to online tools for planning and implementing instruction, and it has excellent segments on libraries, literature, and information literacy. The site also includes online courses.

### Books to Explore

Ashburn, E., & Floden, R. (2006). *Meaningful learning using technology: What educators need to know and do.* New York, NY: Teachers College Press.

Morrison, G. R., & Lowther, D. L. (2005). *Integrating computer technology into the classroom* (3rd ed.). Upper Saddle River, NJ: Merrill.

Smaldino, S. E., Lowther, D. L., & Russell, J. D. (2008). *Instructional technology and media for learning* (9th ed.). Upper Saddle River, NJ: Pearson Prentice Hall.

### Journals

*Media & Methods Magazine* (http://www.media-methods.com/)

*The Journal* (http://thejournal.com/)

*Tech & Learning* (http://www.techlearning.com/)

*New Media* (http://www.newmedia.org/)

## PUBLISHERS

### A. W. Peller

http://www.awpeller.com/

A. W. Peller and Associates has served the educational community for more than three decades, distributing resources for more than 100 publishers, producers, and manufacturers of educational materials. The catalog Bright Ideas for the Gifted and Talented includes a wealth of sources—activity books (all subjects), science/social studies kits, literature guides, critical- and creative-thinking materials for students, teachers, and parents.

## Cobblestone & Cricket (Divisions of Carus Publishing)

www.cobblestonepub.com/resources.html

This publisher provides a number of exceptional and well-loved magazines for young readers of all ages—easy to use in any classroom, library, or home learning program. The New Performance Standards for English Language Arts in Middle School have included *COBBLESTONE, CALLIOPE, FACES,* and *ODYSSEY* in the recommended reading list.

## Corwin

http://www.corwin.com/home.nav

Established in 1990 as an affiliate of SAGE Publications, Corwin has much to offer teachers seeking fresh ideas and practical guidance on meeting the educational needs of advanced students. Its published works provide a much-needed balance between theory and practice and between current research studies and the living classroom. Corwin continues to expand its resources for teachers of gifted learners while providing a wide range of practice-oriented publications for PreK–12 education professionals of all kinds.

## Creative Learning Press

www.creativelearningpress.com

This press provides a rich variety of practical manuals and activity books for teachers working with advanced children. It offers a helpful Mentors-in-Print section with a variety of how-to books that put students in the shoes of practicing professionals in different fields. The books teach real-world skills and methods that young people can use to develop their projects and interests.

## Gifted Education Press

http://www.giftededpress.com/

With 15,000 subscribers, this extraordinary online publisher offers a wide range of articles by prominent educators on identifying and educating advanced students, dating back to 1987. The subscription is complimentary. In addition, a discussion group on problems and issues related to meeting the educational needs of this neglected population provides an excellent forum for teachers to pool their experience and resources.

## Pieces of Learning

www.piecesoflearning.com

A Division of Creative Learning Consultants, Pieces of Learning publishes and produces outstanding books and materials on a wide range of subjects and topics from some of the most popular authors in the field. The site offers information on differentiation, critical and creative thinking, questioning skills, as well as innovative materials for subjects such as literature, writing, math, science, thematic learning, research, and much more.

## Prufrock Press

www.prufrock.com

Prufrock is a publisher of innovative products and materials that support the education of gifted and talented children. It also provides teachers and parents with a comprehensive online education resource, a listing of useful links and products, gifted education magazines (e.g. *Gifted Child Today*), research journals, identification instruments, books, and more.

# References

Advocate. (n.d.). In *The Free Dictionary* online dictionary. Retrieved from http://www.thefreedictionary.com/advocate.

Ames, C. A. (1990, Spring). Motivation: What teachers need to know. *Teachers College Record, 91,* 409–421.

Anderson, L. W., & Krathwohl, D. R. (Eds.). (2001). *A taxonomy for learning, teaching, and assessing: A revision of Bloom's taxonomy of educational objectives.* New York, NY: Longman.

Bailiwick. (n.d.). *In OxFord's online English dictionary.* Retrieved from http://www.oxforddictionaries.com/definition/bailiwick?view=uk.

Barrows, H. S. (1997). Problem-based learning is more than just learning based around problems. *The Problem Log, 2*(2), 4–5.

Christensen, J. (1996). *The art of James Christensen: A journey of the imagination.* Seymour, CT: The Greenwich Workshop Press.

Colangelo, N., Assouline, S., & Gross, M. (2004). *A nation deceived: How schools hold back America's brightest students. The Templeton national report on acceleration.* Iowa City: The University of Iowa.

Daniels, S., & Piechowski, M. M. (2009). *Living with intensity: Understanding the sensitivity, excitability and emotional development of gifted children, adolescents and adults.* Scottsdale, AZ: Great Potential Press.

Emerson, R.W. (2007). *Collected works of Ralph Waldo Emerson—volume II—essays: First series.* (J. Slater & A.R. Ferguson, eds.). Cambridge, MA: Harvard University Press.

Fleming, V. (Director). (1939). *The wizard of oz* [Motion picture].USA: MGM.

Flack, J. (2000). The gifted reader in the regular classroom: Strategies for success. *Illinois Association for Gifted Children Journal,* 22–30.

Freeman, C. (2003). Designing math curriculum to encourage inductive thinking by elementary and middle school students. In J. F. Smutny (Ed.), *Designing and developing programs for gifted students* (pp. 69–85). Thousand Oaks: Corwin.

Gardner, H. (1993). *Frames of mind: The theory of multiple intelligences.* New York, NY: Basic Books.

Gardner, H. (1999). *Intelligence reframed: Multiple intelligences for the 21st century.* New York, NY: Basic Books.

Guilford, J. P. (1968). *Intelligence, creativity, and their educational implications.* San Diego, CA: Robert R. Knapp.

Heacox, D. (2002). *Differentiating instruction in the regular classroom: How to reach and teach all learners, Grades 3–12.* Minneapolis: Free Spirit Press.

Herring, J. (n.d.). *Inspiration for teachers: 8 universal laws.* Retrieved from Ezine Articles, http://ezinearticles.com/?Inspiration-for-Teachers:—8-Universal-Laws&id=69044.

hooks, bell. (1990). *Yearning: Race, gender, and cultural politics.* Boston, MA: South End Press.

Kulik, J. A., & Kulik, C. L. C. (1990). Ability grouping and gifted students. In N. Colangelo & G. Davis (Eds.), *Handbook of gifted education,* pp. 178–196. Boston, MA: Allyn & Bacon.

Lind, S. (2001). Overexcitability and the gifted. *The SENG Newsletter, 1*(1), 3–6.

Locker, T., & Christensen, C. (2001). *Sky tree: Seeing science through art.* New York, NY: HarperCollins.

Math Academy Online. (2011). *The mathematic art of M. C. Escher.* Retrieved from http://www.mathacademy.com/pr/minitext/escher.

Morrison, T. (1996). *The dancing mind.* New York, NY: Alfred A. Knopf.

Nash, D. (2001, December). Enter the mentor. *Parenting for High Potential,* 18–21.

National Council of Teacher of Mathematics (NCTM). (2011). *Standards and focal points.* Retrieved from http://www.nctm.org/standards/default.aspx?id=58.

Ogle, D. M. (1986). K-W-L: A teaching model that develops active reading of expository text. *Reading Teacher, 39,* 564–570.

Schrag, P. (2000, August). High stakes are for tomatoes. *The Atlantic Monthly, 286*(2), 19–21.

Siegle, D., & McCoach, D. B. (2005). Extending learning through mentorships. In F. A. Karnes & S. M. Bean (Eds.), *Methods and materials for teaching the gifted* (2nd ed., pp. 473–518). Waco, TX: Prufrock Press.

Smutny, J. F. (2007). *Reclaiming the lives of gifted girls and women.* Unionville, NY: Royal Fireworks Press.

Smutny, J. F., & von Fremd, S. E. (2009). *Igniting creativity in gifted learners, K–6: Strategies for every teacher.* Thousand Oaks, CA: Corwin.

Smutny, J. F., & von Fremd, S. E. (2010). *Differentiating for the young child: Teaching strategies across the content areas, PreK–3* (2nd ed.). Thousand Oaks, CA: Corwin.

Smutny, J. F., Walker, S. Y., & Meckstroth, E. A. (1997). *Teaching young gifted children in the regular classroom.* Minneapolis, MN: Free Spirit.

Smutny, J. F., Walker, S. Y., & Meckstroth, E. A. (2007). *Acceleration for gifted learners, K–5.* Thousand Oaks, CA: Corwin.

Subotnik, R. (1995). Talent developed: Conversations with masters of the arts and sciences. *Journal for the Education of the Gifted, 18*(2), 210–226.

Thompson, M. C. (2000, March 7). *Curriculum as profound engagement with the world.* Keynote speech to the National Curriculum Networking Conference, The College of William and Mary, Williamsburg, Virginia.

Tompert, A. (1990). *Grandfather Tang's story: A tale told with tangrams.* New York, NY: Crown.

Torrance, E. P. (1974). *Torrance tests of creative thinking: Norms and technical manual.* Lexington, MA: Personnel Press.

Torrance, E. P. (1979). *The search for satori and creativity.* Buffalo, NY: Creative Education Foundation.

Torrance, E. P. (1980). Growing up creatively gifted: A 22-year longitudinal study. *Creative Child and Adult Quarterly, 5*(3), 148–158, 170.

Torrance, E. P. (1983). The importance of falling in love with "something." *Creative Child and Adult Quarterly, 8*(2), 72–78.

Turner, D. (2009, Sunday, November 22). Less funding for gifted students. *The Washington Times.* Retrieved March 10, 2010, from http://www .washingtontimes.com/news/2009/nov/22/gifted-students-are-being-left -behind-in-funding-r/?page=1.

Van Allsburg, C. (1996). *The mysteries of Harris Burdick* (Portfolio Edition). Boston, MA: Houghton Mifflin Harcourt.

Wiggins, G., & McTighe, J. (2001). *Understanding by design.* Upper Saddle River, NJ: Prentice Hall.

Winebrenner, S., & Devlin, B. (2001, March). *Cluster grouping of gifted students: How to provide full-time services on a part-time budget.* Educational Research Information Center (ERIC E607). Retrieved from http://www.hoagiesgifted .org/eric/e607.html.

# Index

**CORWIN**
A SAGE Company

The Corwin logo—a raven striding across an open book—represents the union of courage and learning. Corwin is committed to improving education for all learners by publishing books and other professional development resources for those serving the field of PreK–12 education. By providing practical, hands-on materials, Corwin continues to carry out the promise of its motto: **"Helping Educators Do Their Work Better."**